T0155298

JUMBLE® Jubilee

A Party of Puzzles

by Henri Arnold, Bob Lee, and Mike Argirion

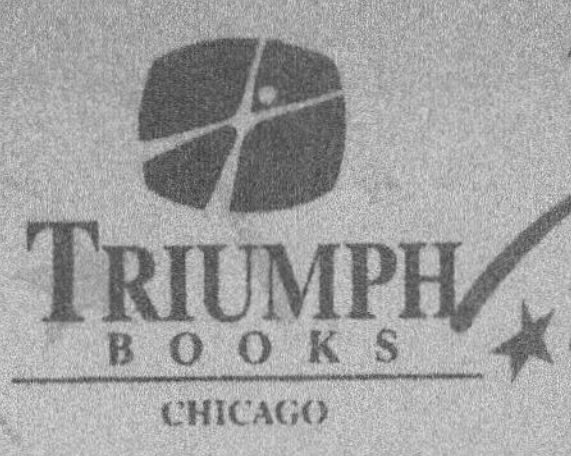

TRIUMPH BOOKS
CHICAGO

This book is available at special discounts
for your group or organization.

For further information, contact:

Triumph Books LLC
814 North Franklin Street
Chicago, IL 60610
(800) 888-4741
(312) 337-1807 FAX

ISBN 1-57243-231-4

Printed in the USA

ISBN 978-1-57243-231-4

CONTENTS

CLASSIC
JUMBLE
Jubilee

JUMBLE®

Unscramble these four Jumbles, one letter to each square, to form four ordinary words.

YURLT

SHWIK

ONASAT

TEVVLE

WHAT GOLD DIGGERS GO FOR IN ORDER TO GET DIAMONDS.

Now arrange the circled letters to form the surprise answer, as suggested by the above cartoon.

Print the SURPRISE ANSWER here

2

JUMBLE®

Unscramble these four Jumbles, one letter to each square, to form four ordinary words.

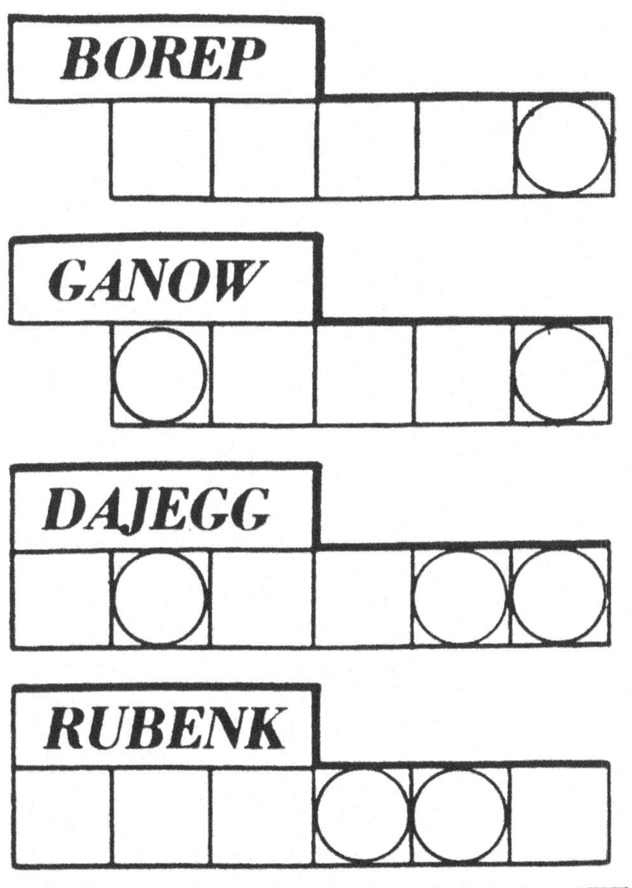
BOREP
GANOW
DAJEGG
RUBENK

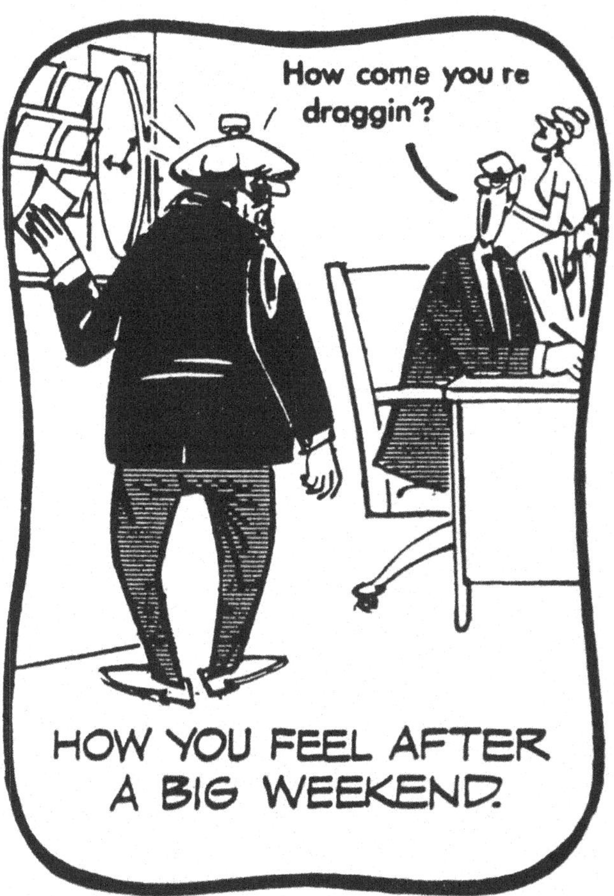
How come you're draggin'?
HOW YOU FEEL AFTER A BIG WEEKEND.

Now arrange the circled letters to form the surprise answer, as suggested by the above cartoon.

Print the SURPRISE ANSWER here

JUMBLE®

Unscramble these four Jumbles, one letter to each square, to form four ordinary words.

PORRI

WENIT

PEXLUD

MANDOR

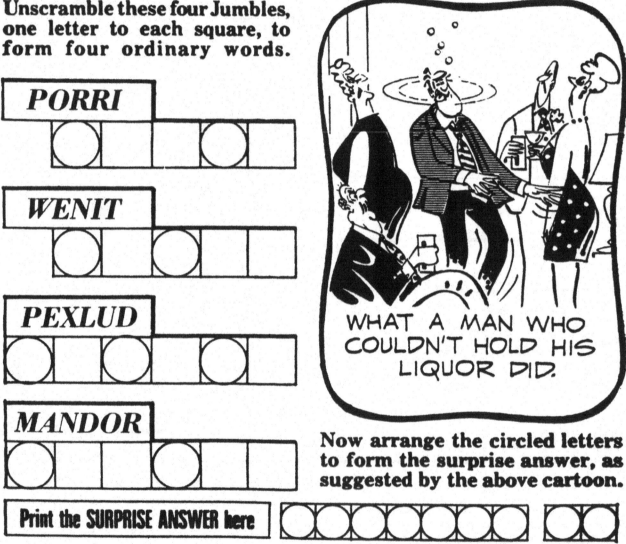

WHAT A MAN WHO COULDN'T HOLD HIS LIQUOR DID.

Now arrange the circled letters to form the surprise answer, as suggested by the above cartoon.

Print the SURPRISE ANSWER here

4

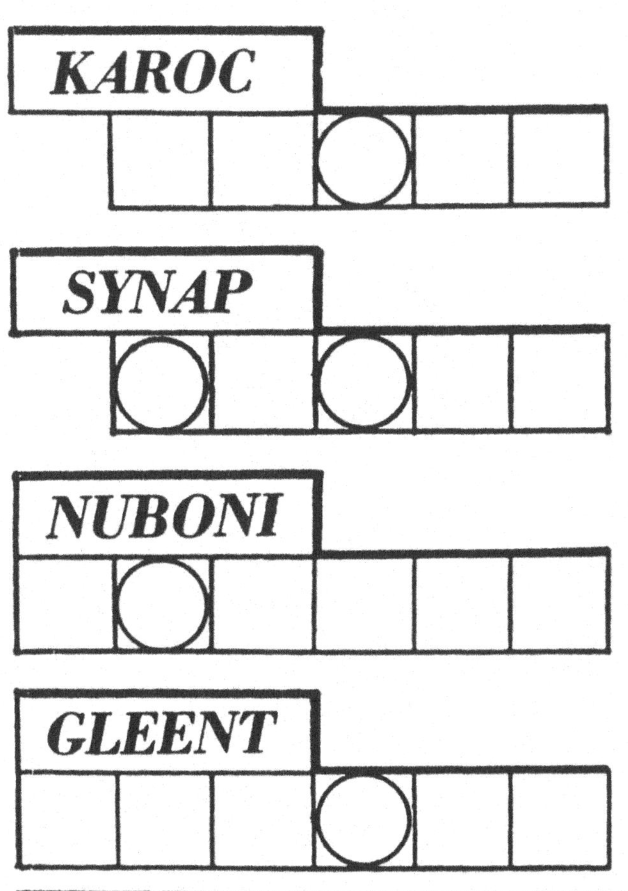

JUMBLE®

Unscramble these four Jumbles, one letter to each square, to form four ordinary words.

KAROC

SYNAP

NUBONI

GLEENT

We want our money back!
WHAT THE NUDE SHOW TURNED OUT TO BE.

Now arrange the circled letters to form the surprise answer, as suggested by the above cartoon.

Print the SURPRISE ANSWER here

A  - 

5

JUMBLE®

Unscramble these four Jumbles, one letter to each square, to form four ordinary words.

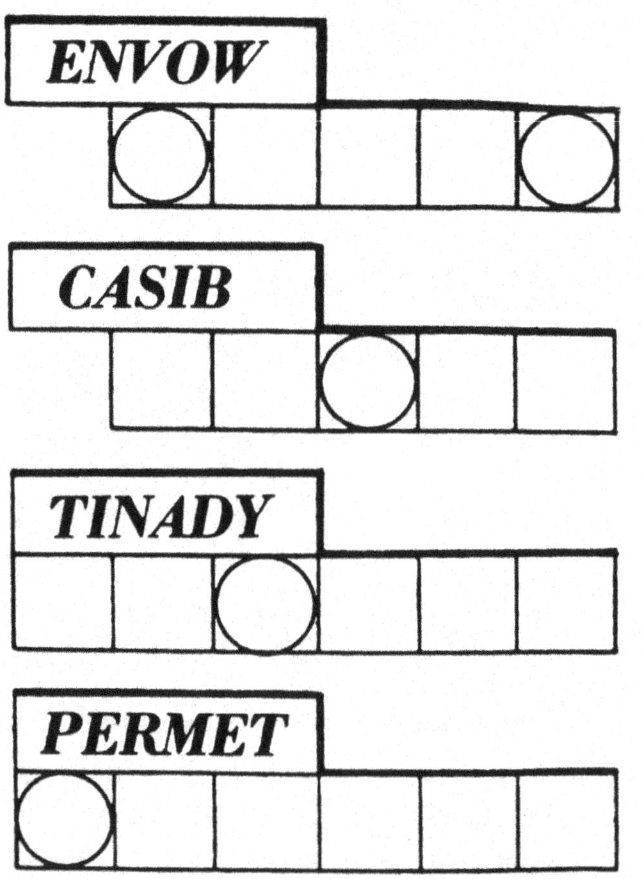
ENVOW
CASIB
TINADY
PERMET

WHAT THE MAN WHO WORE TWO SUITS TO A MASQUERADE PARTY WENT AS.

Now arrange the circled letters to form the surprise answer, as suggested by the above cartoon.

Print the SURPRISE ANSWER here

JUMBLE®

Unscramble these four Jumbles, one letter to each square, to form four ordinary words.

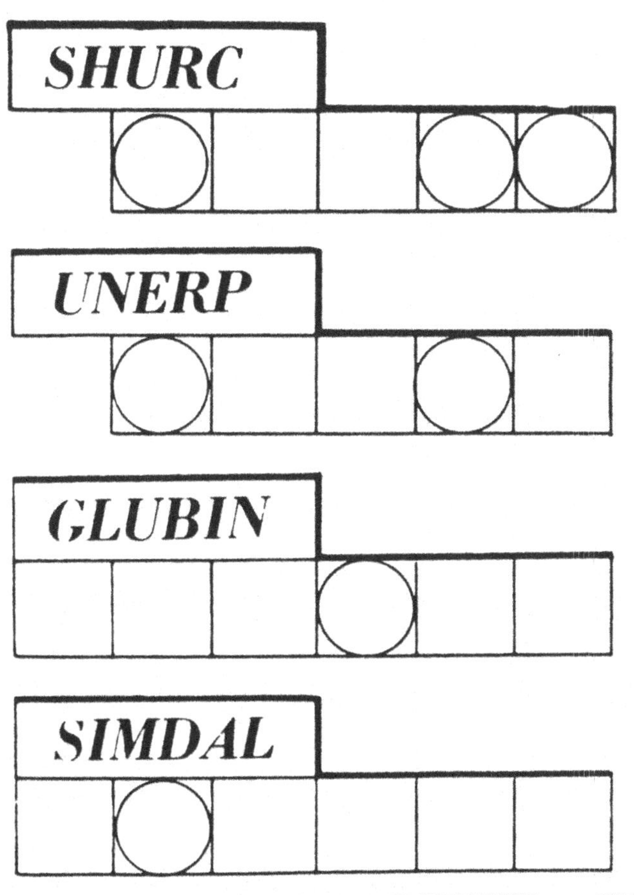

SHURC
UNERP
GLUBIN
SIMDAL

WHEN YOU'RE THIS IT'S EASY TO FEEL CHIPPER.

Now arrange the circled letters to form the surprise answer, as suggested by the above cartoon.

Print the SURPRISE ANSWER here 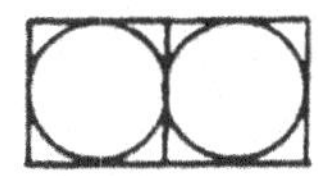 **THE** 

7

JUMBLE®

Unscramble these four Jumbles, one letter to each square, to form four ordinary words.

PIPNY

TUNDA

GUMSED

DUTOXE

NOW PLAYING

WHAT THE BURLESQUE QUEEN WAS RESPONSIBLE FOR.

Now arrange the circled letters to form the surprise answer, as suggested by the above cartoon.

Print the SURPRISE ANSWER here

HER OWN " "

8

JUMBLE®

Unscramble these four Jumbles, one letter to each square, to form four ordinary words.

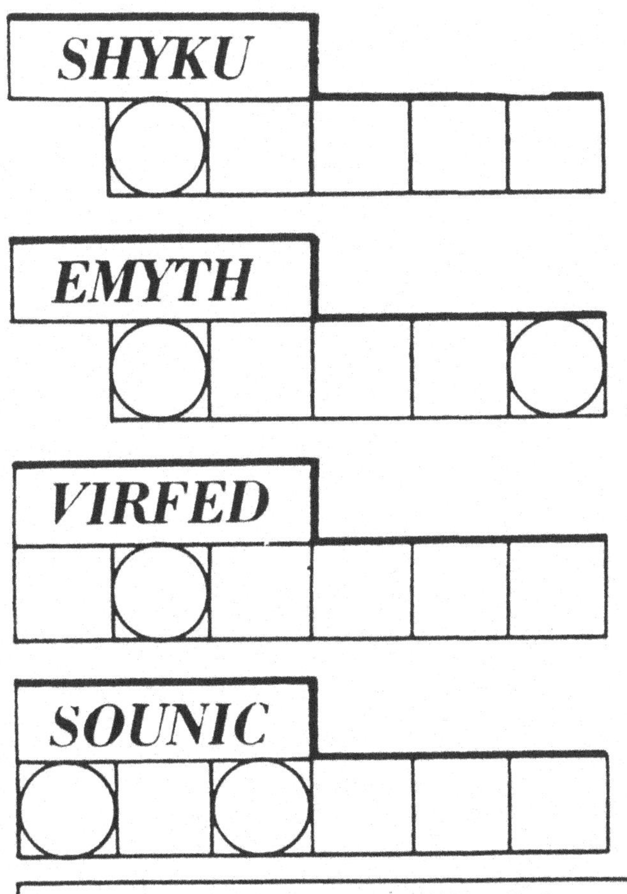
SHYKU
EMYTH
VIRFED
SOUNIC

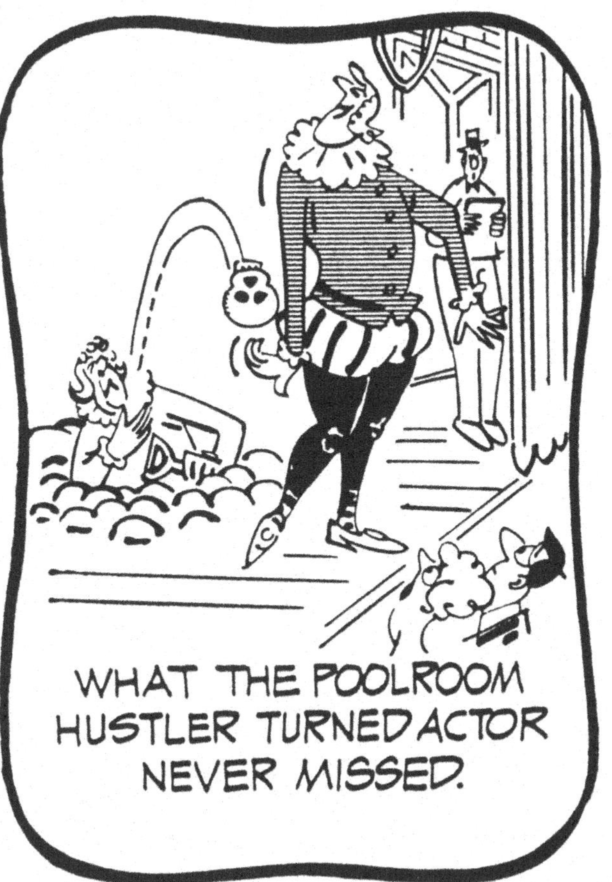

WHAT THE POOLROOM HUSTLER TURNED ACTOR NEVER MISSED.

Now arrange the circled letters to form the surprise answer, as suggested by the above cartoon.

Print the SURPRISE ANSWER here

9

JUMBLE®

Unscramble these four Jumbles, one letter to each square, to form four ordinary words.

YEDEK

RIVOY

SPITTY

YALMIN

GOWNS

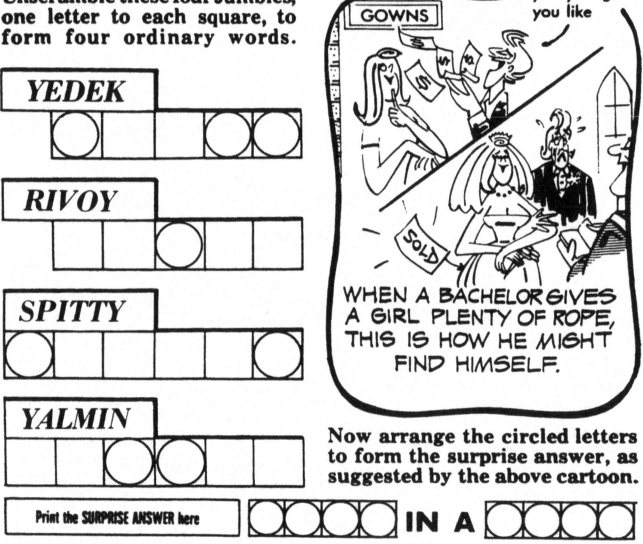

Buy anything you like

SOLD

WHEN A BACHELOR GIVES A GIRL PLENTY OF ROPE, THIS IS HOW HE MIGHT FIND HIMSELF.

Now arrange the circled letters to form the surprise answer, as suggested by the above cartoon.

Print the SURPRISE ANSWER here

IN A

10

JUMBLE®

Unscramble these four Jumbles, one letter to each square, to form four ordinary words.

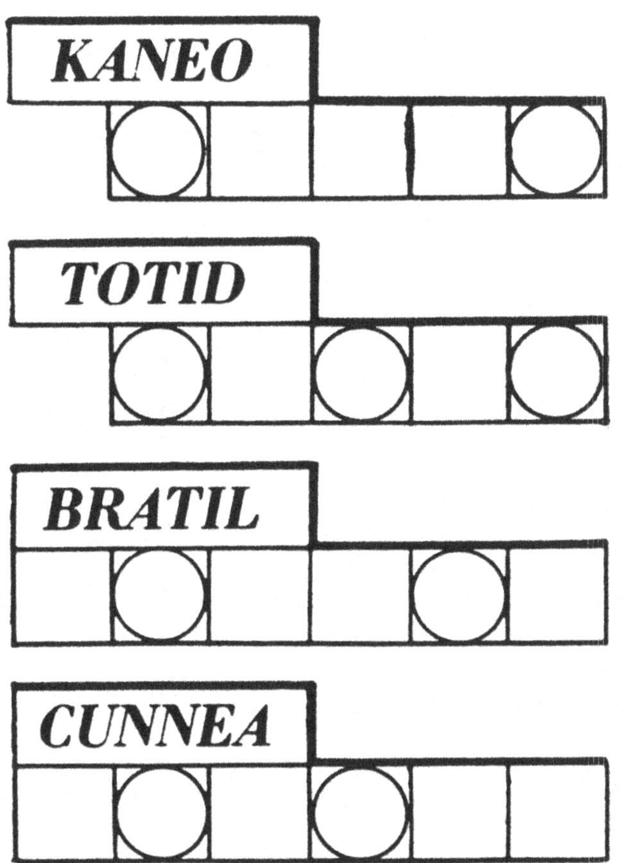
KANEO
TOTID
BRATIL
CUNNEA

How old? — Shhh!
THE BEST WAY TO TELL A WOMAN'S AGE.

Now arrange the circled letters to form the surprise answer, as suggested by the above cartoon.

ANSWER here **WHEN SHE'S**  

11

JUMBLE®

Unscramble these four Jumbles, one letter to each square, to form four ordinary words.

LIEBE

☐☐☐☐◯

DILEY

☐☐☐☐◯

BINNOR

☐☐◯☐☐☐

TAIGER

☐☐◯☐☐◯

THIS MIGHT BE THE LATEST THING IN WEDDINGS!

TV

Now arrange the circled letters to form the surprise answer, as suggested by the above cartoon.

Print the SURPRISE ANSWER here

THE ◯◯◯◯◯

12

JUMBLE®

Unscramble these four Jumbles, one letter to each square, to form four ordinary words.

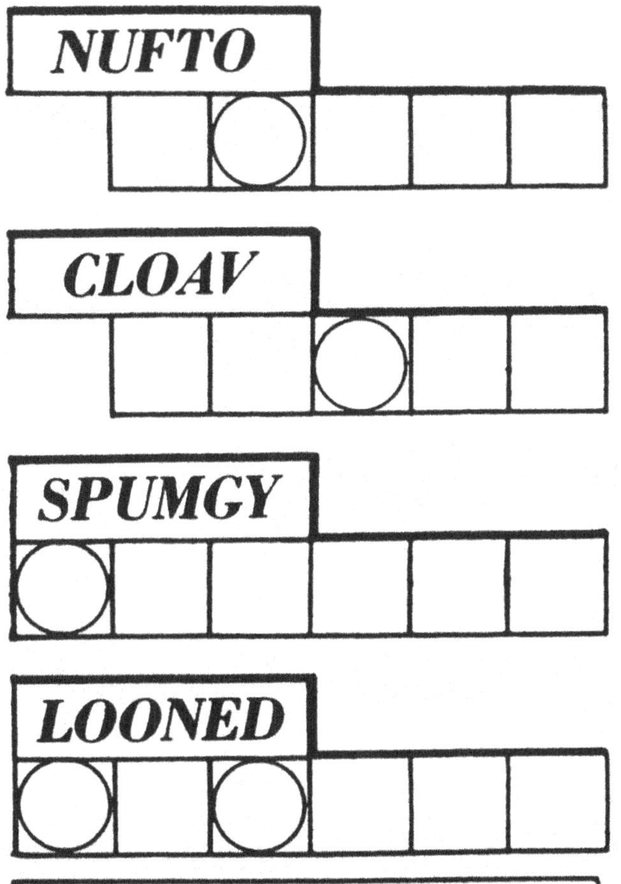
NUFTO
CLOAV
SPUMGY
LOONED

WHAT THEY DANCED DURING THE PRISON BREAK.

Now arrange the circled letters to form the surprise answer, as suggested by the above cartoon.

Print the SURPRISE ANSWER here

THE "◯◯◯-◯◯"

13

JUMBLE®

Unscramble these four Jumbles, one letter to each square, to form four ordinary words.

TIBEF

KARIF

DOALUN

SOUMUC

She was a knockout

WHAT HAPPENED TO THE GIRL WITH THE HOURGLASS FIGURE?

Now arrange the circled letters to form the surprise answer, as suggested by the above cartoon.

Print the SURPRISE ANSWER here ◯◯◯◯ ◯◯◯ **OUT**

14

JUMBLE®

Unscramble these four Jumbles, one letter to each square, to form four ordinary words.

LUMGO

TUGYO

LEWVIE

TESACK

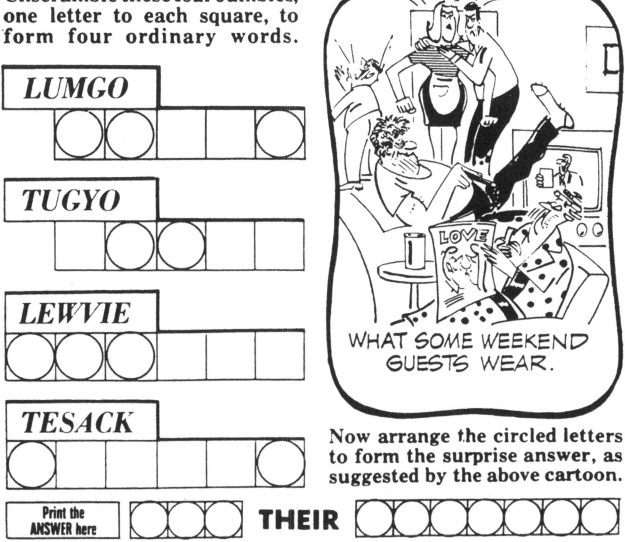

WHAT SOME WEEKEND GUESTS WEAR.

Now arrange the circled letters to form the surprise answer, as suggested by the above cartoon.

Print the ANSWER here

THEIR

15

JUMBLE®

Unscramble these four Jumbles, one letter to each square, to form four ordinary words.

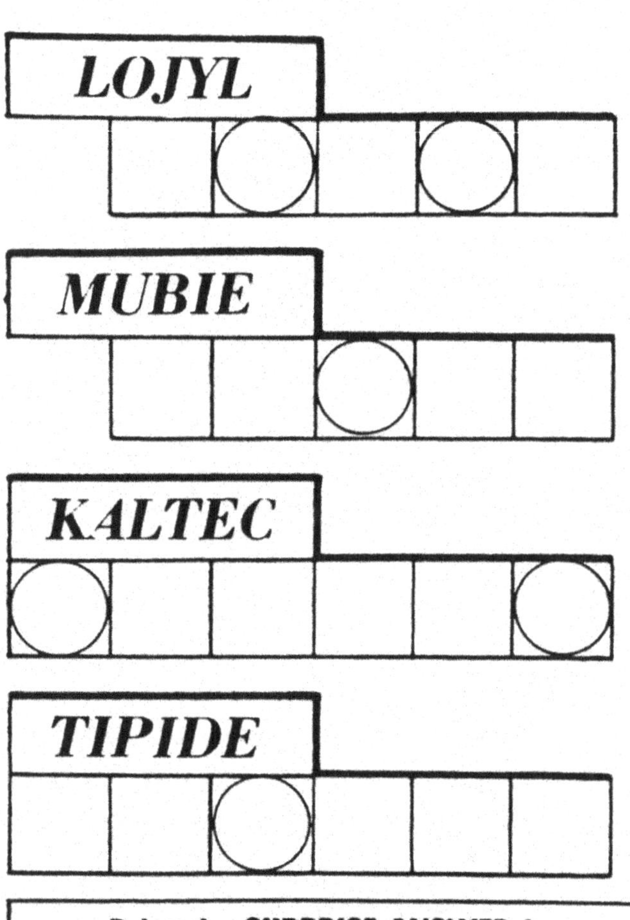

LOJYL
MUBIE
KALTEC
TIPIDE

YE TAVERN
CLOSED
WHEN OPEN, IT PROVIDES DRINKS.

Now arrange the circled letters to form the surprise answer, as suggested by the above cartoon.

Print the SURPRISE ANSWER here

A 

16

JUMBLE®

Unscramble these four Jumbles, one letter to each square, to form four ordinary words.

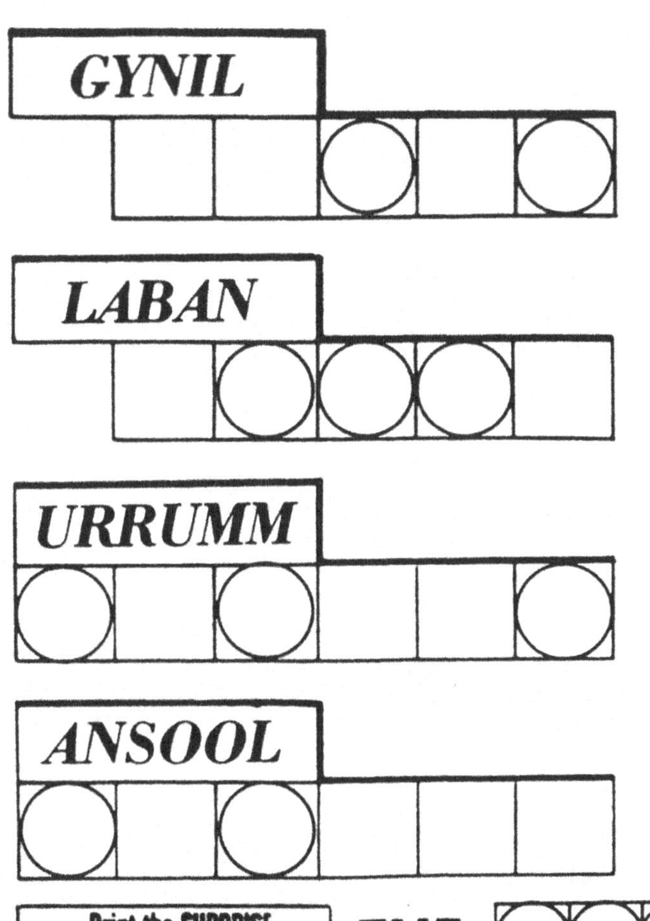
GYNIL
LABAN
URRUMM
ANSOOL

DOWN
WITH
ARISE!
WHEN THIS HAPPENS, YOU MIGHT EXPECT A PREARRANGED UPRISING TO TAKE PLACE.

Now arrange the circled letters to form the surprise answer, as suggested by the above cartoon.

Print the SURPRISE ANSWER here

THE

JUMBLE®

Unscramble these four Jumbles, one letter to each square, to form four ordinary words.

PARPE

KONET

LYNFOD

VISTEN

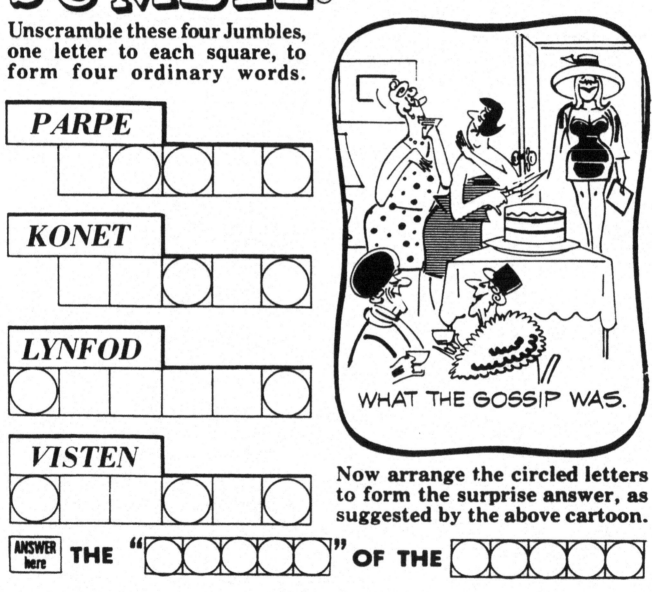

WHAT THE GOSSIP WAS.

Now arrange the circled letters to form the surprise answer, as suggested by the above cartoon.

ANSWER here: **THE "   " OF THE   **

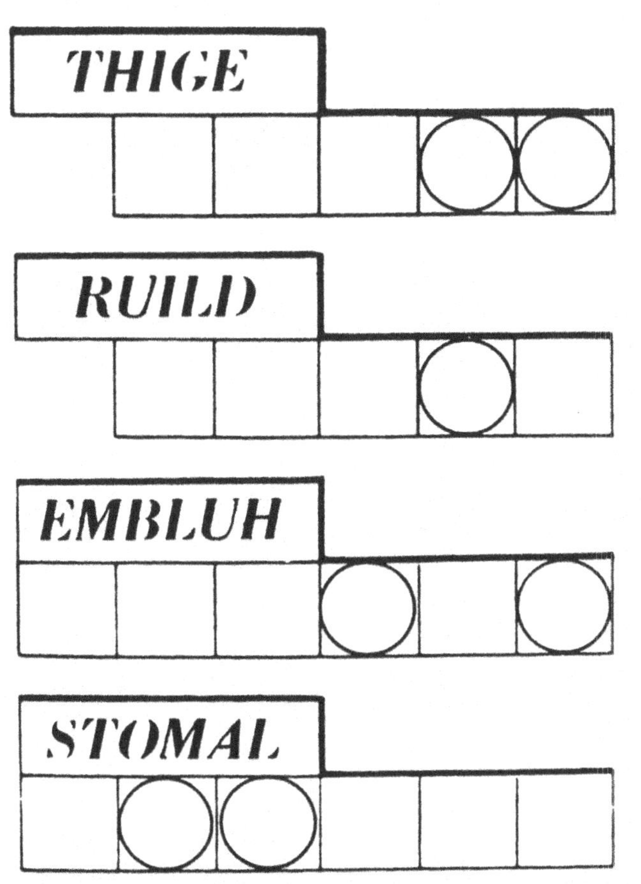
JUMBLE®
Unscramble these four Jumbles, one letter to each square, to form four ordinary words.
THIGE
RUILD
EMBLUH
STOMAL

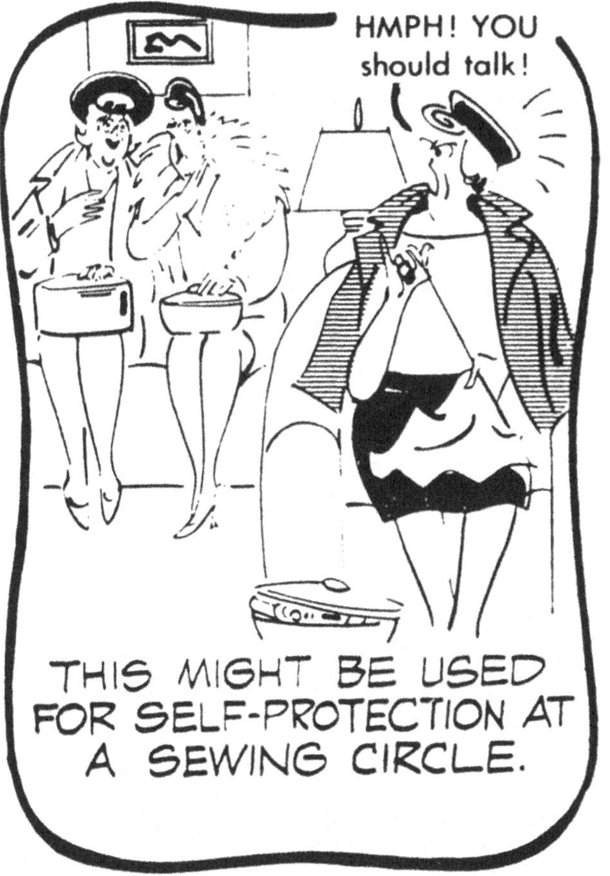
HMPH! YOU should talk!
THIS MIGHT BE USED FOR SELF-PROTECTION AT A SEWING CIRCLE.

Now arrange the circled letters to form the surprise answer, as suggested by the above cartoon.

Print the SURPRISE ANSWER here

A 

JUMBLE®

Unscramble these four Jumbles, one letter to each square, to form four ordinary words.

DALGE

PANCO

REFOBE

MULVLE

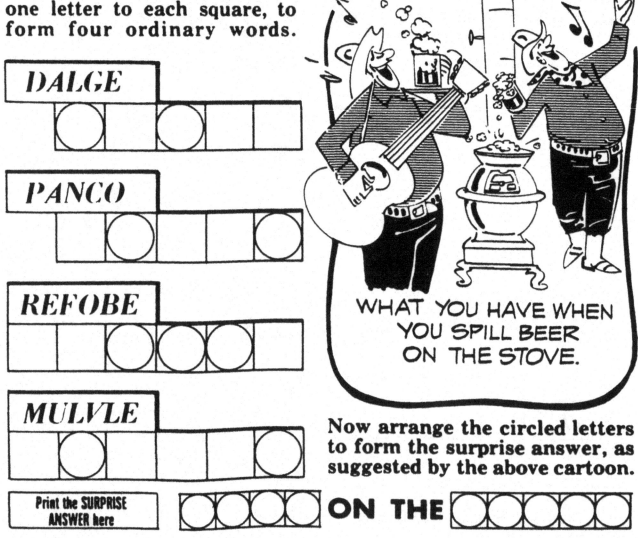

WHAT YOU HAVE WHEN YOU SPILL BEER ON THE STOVE.

Now arrange the circled letters to form the surprise answer, as suggested by the above cartoon.

Print the SURPRISE ANSWER here

ON THE

20

JUMBLE®

Unscramble these four Jumbles, one letter to each square, to form four ordinary words.

LEETA

ASTUE

WYIHNN

KOHOED

WHILE
-U-
WAIT

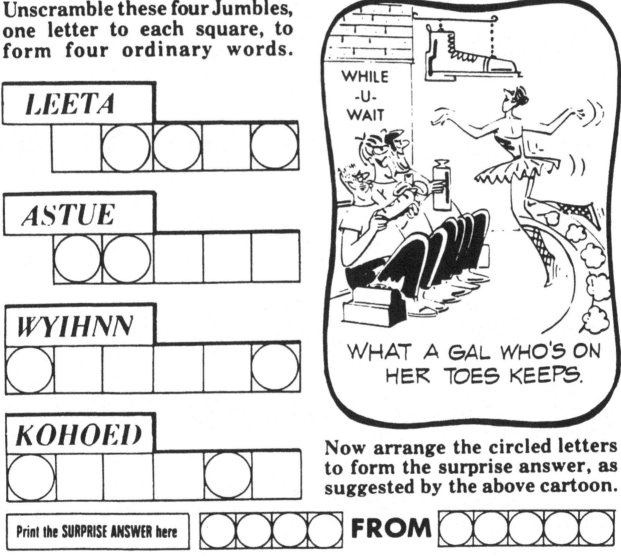

WHAT A GAL WHO'S ON HER TOES KEEPS.

Now arrange the circled letters to form the surprise answer, as suggested by the above cartoon.

Print the SURPRISE ANSWER here

FROM

21

JUMBLE®

Unscramble these four Jumbles, one letter to each square, to form four ordinary words.

KEREC

DULEE

TECJOB

GOLLAB

Dear!

WHY HE COULDN'T TELL THAT JOKE ABOUT OIL.

Now arrange the circled letters to form the surprise answer, as suggested by the above cartoon.

Print the SURPRISE ANSWER here **IT WAS**

22

JUMBLE®

Unscramble these four Jumbles, one letter to each square, to form four ordinary words.

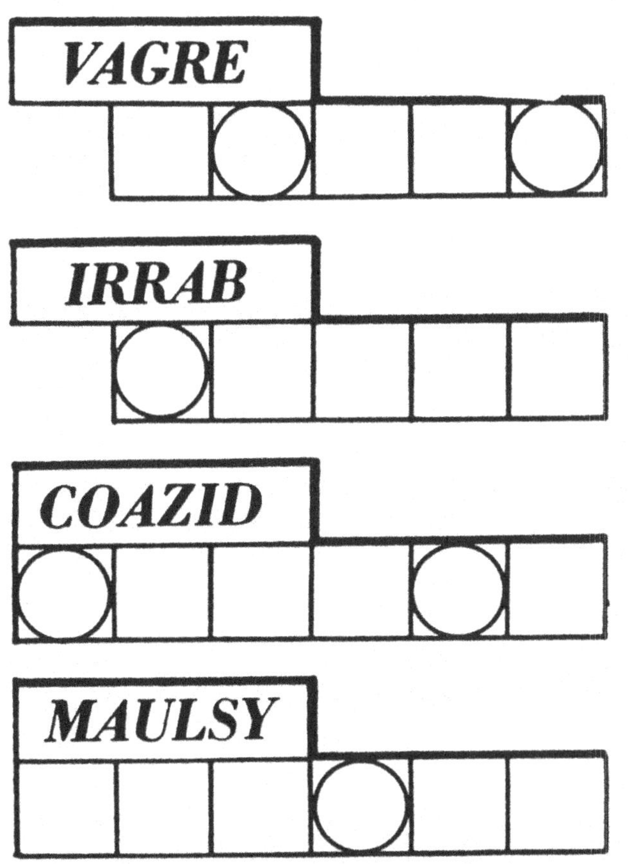
VAGRE
IRRAB
COAZID
MAULSY

Quick! The hose!
WHAT THE JACKET THAT CAUGHT FIRE MUST HAVE BEEN.

Now arrange the circled letters to form the surprise answer, as suggested by the above cartoon.

Print the SURPRISE ANSWER here

A

23

JUMBLE®

Unscramble these four Jumbles, one letter to each square, to form four ordinary words.

MIRPE

RUZEA

GENPOS

PEEXOS

Hmph!

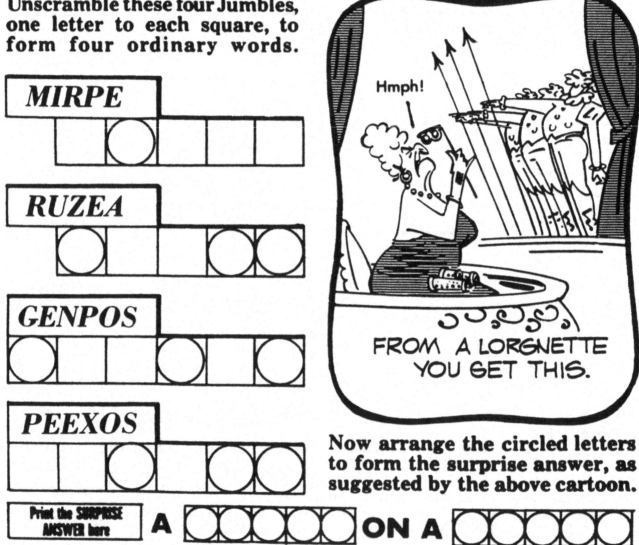

FROM A LORGNETTE YOU GET THIS.

Now arrange the circled letters to form the surprise answer, as suggested by the above cartoon.

Print the SURPRISE ANSWER here

A ◯◯◯◯◯ ON A ◯◯◯◯◯

JUMBLE®

Unscramble these four Jumbles, one letter to each square, to form four ordinary words.

NACAL

IMERG

RODIAH

SMEECH

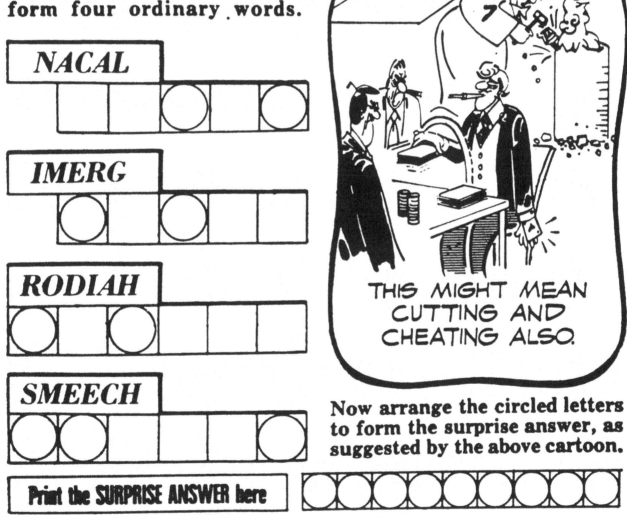

THIS MIGHT MEAN CUTTING AND CHEATING ALSO.

Now arrange the circled letters to form the surprise answer, as suggested by the above cartoon.

Print the SURPRISE ANSWER here

JUMBLE®

Unscramble these four Jumbles, one letter to each square, to form four ordinary words.

UPDYM

CHABT

SMALEY

VOINEC

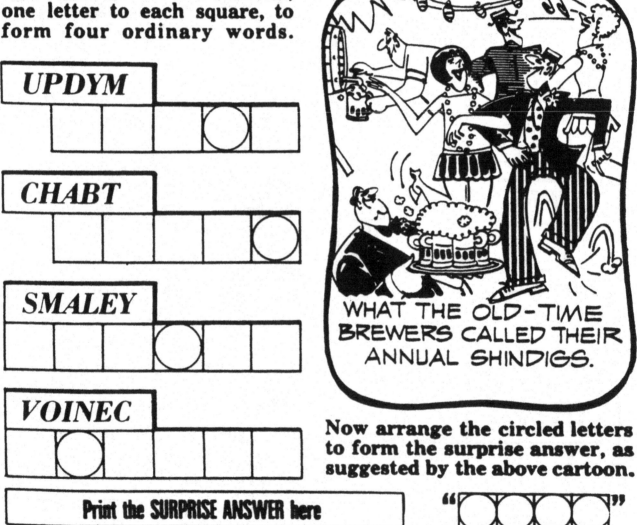

WHAT THE OLD-TIME BREWERS CALLED THEIR ANNUAL SHINDIGS.

Now arrange the circled letters to form the surprise answer, as suggested by the above cartoon.

Print the SURPRISE ANSWER here

“ ”

26

JUMBLE®

Unscramble these four Jumbles, one letter to each square, to form four ordinary words.

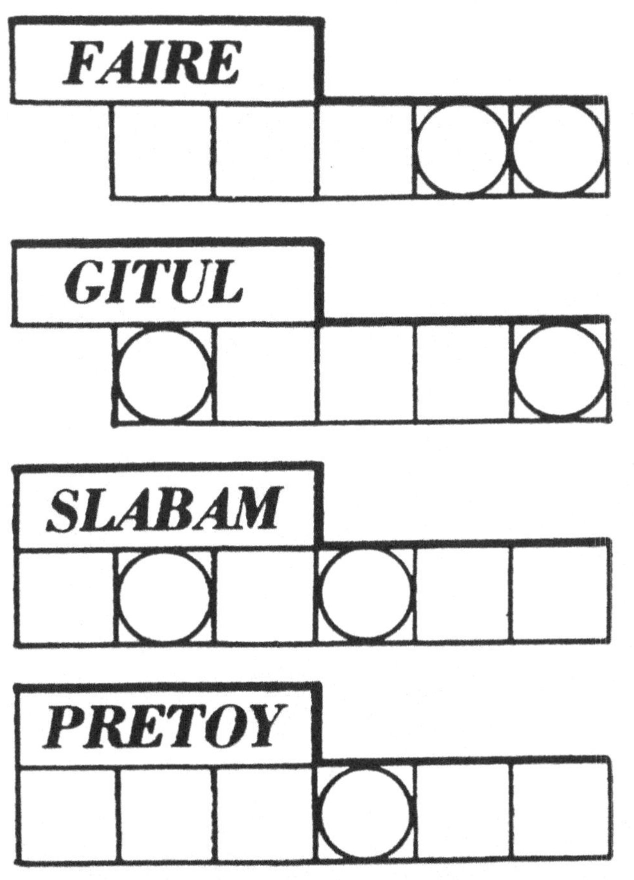
FAIRE
GITUL
SLABAM
PRETOY

Your drink, sir
Marksman?
WHAT YOU MIGHT AIM FOR IN SOME CIRCLES.

Now arrange the circled letters to form the surprise answer, as suggested by the above cartoon.

Print the SURPRISE ANSWER here

27

JUMBLE®
Unscramble these four Jumbles, one letter to each square, to form four ordinary words.
DABNY
KARAP
RIVLIE
HYBBUC

That'll be a buck
WHAT PEOPLE WHO DRINK TO FORGET SHOULD DO.

Now arrange the circled letters to form the surprise answer, as suggested by the above cartoon.

Print the SURPRISE ANSWER here

IN

JUMBLE®

Unscramble these four Jumbles, one letter to each square, to form four ordinary words.

HACTY

SYNIO

RUGEDD

FLUBEM

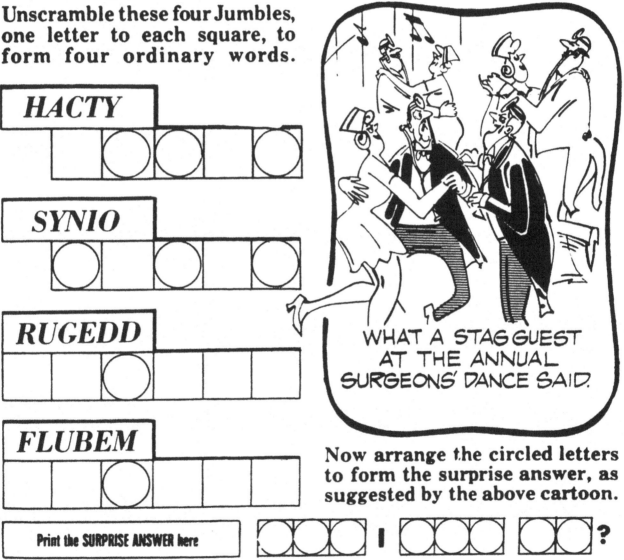

WHAT A STAG GUEST AT THE ANNUAL SURGEONS' DANCE SAID.

Now arrange the circled letters to form the surprise answer, as suggested by the above cartoon.

Print the SURPRISE ANSWER here

I ?

29

JUMBLE®

Unscramble these four Jumbles, one letter to each square, to form four ordinary words.

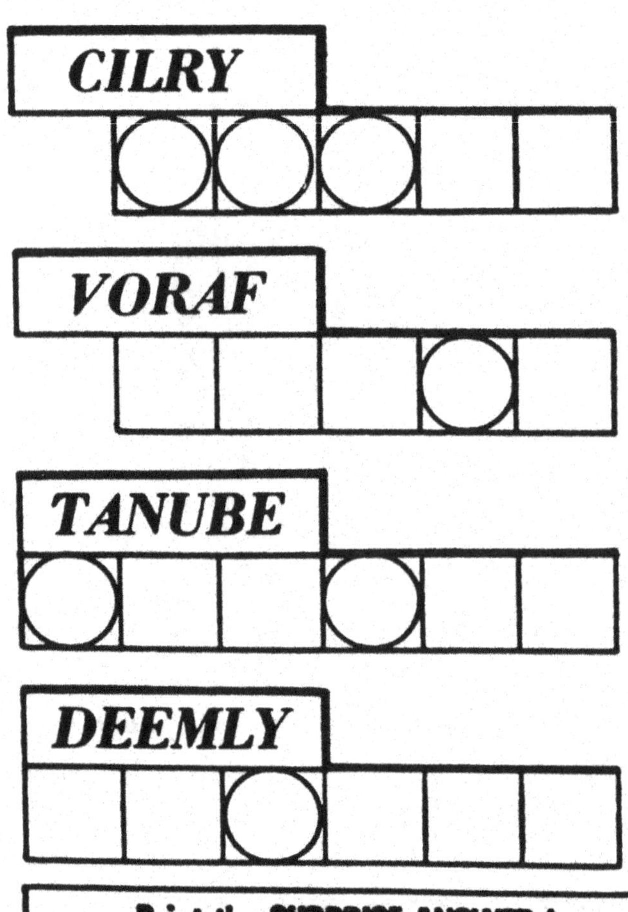
CILRY
VORAF
TANUBE
DEEMLY

I love 'em all!
HOW THE FAT MAN SPOKE.

Now arrange the circled letters to form the surprise answer, as suggested by the above cartoon.

Print the SURPRISE ANSWER here

30

JUMBLE®

Unscramble these four Jumbles, one letter to each square, to form four ordinary words.

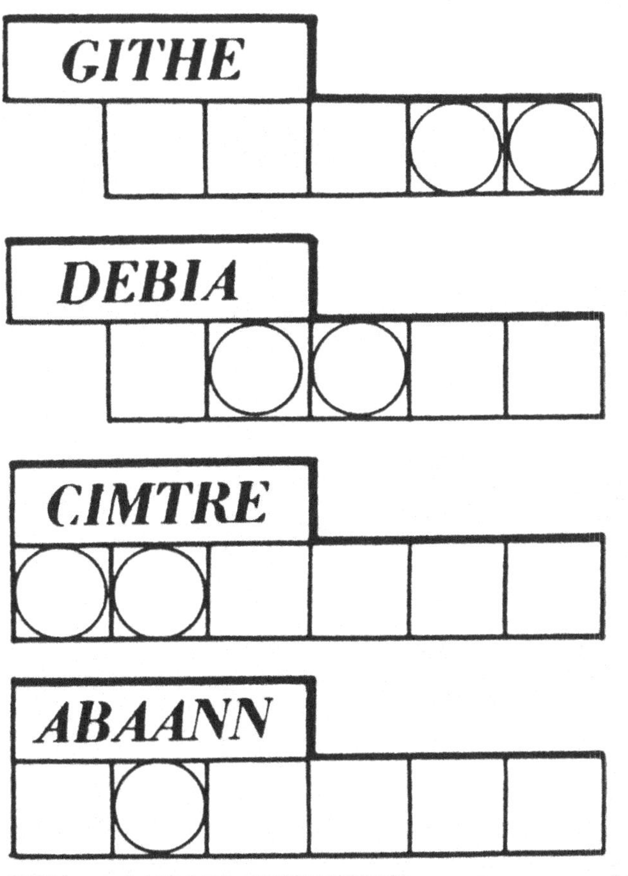
GITHE
DEBIA
CIMTRE
ABAANN

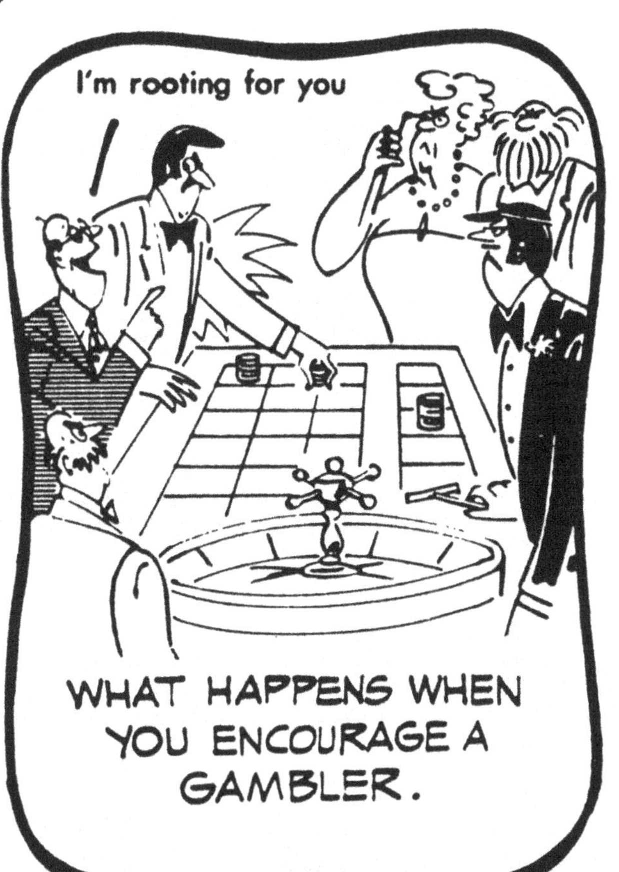
I'm rooting for you
WHAT HAPPENS WHEN YOU ENCOURAGE A GAMBLER.

Now arrange the circled letters to form the surprise answer, as suggested by the above cartoon.

Print the SURPRISE ANSWER here:

YOU “ - ”

31

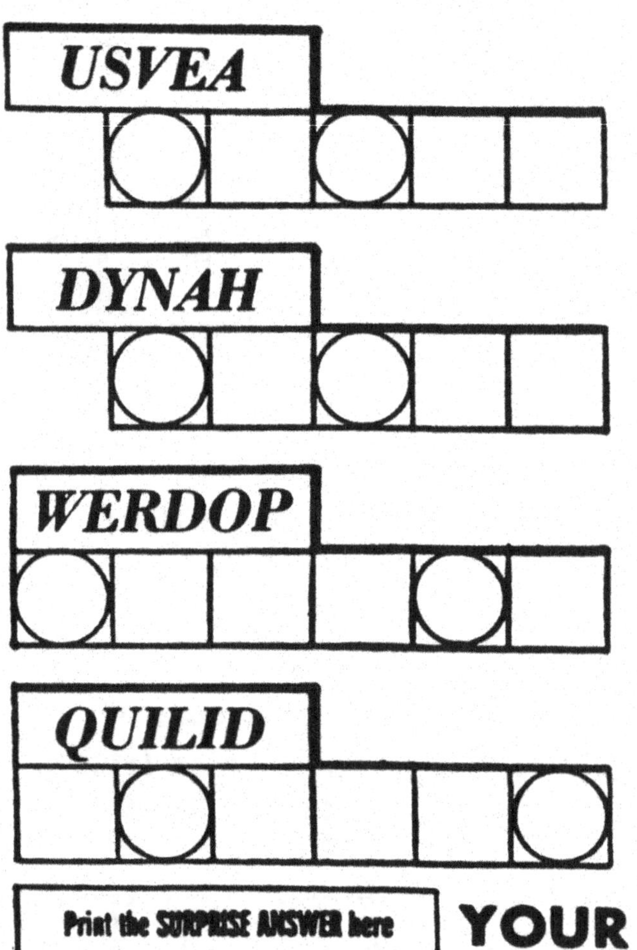
JUMBLE®
Unscramble these four Jumbles, one letter to each square, to form four ordinary words.
USVEA
DYNAH
WERDOP
QUILID

WHAT A TOP HAT
MIGHT MAKE.

Now arrange the circled letters to form the surprise answer, as suggested by the above cartoon.

Print the SURPRISE ANSWER here **YOUR**

32

JUMBLE®

Unscramble these four Jumbles, one letter to each square, to form four ordinary words.

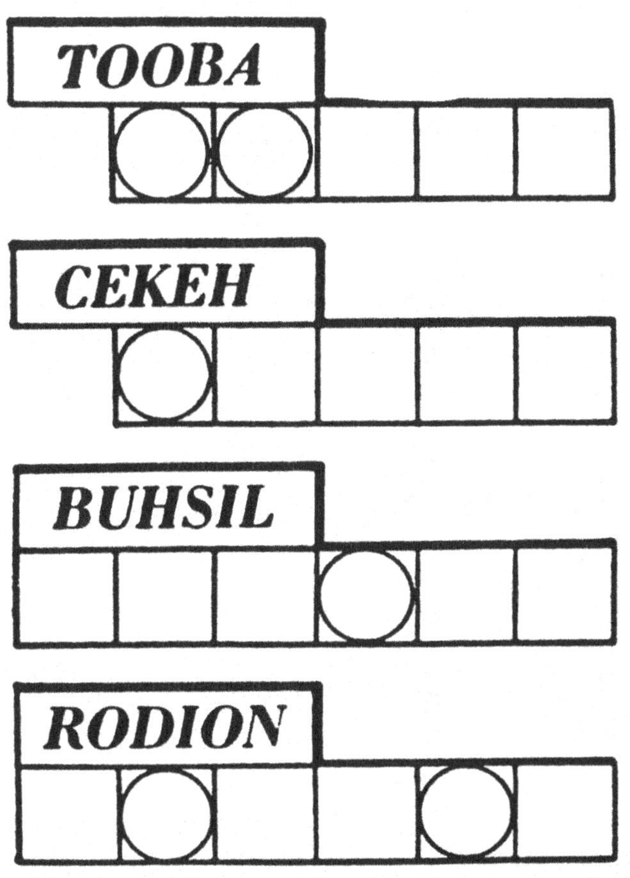
TOOBA
CEKEH
BUHSIL
RODION

DANCE
Not that dull place!
IF IT'S STILL THERE, THERE ISN'T ANY.

Now arrange the circled letters to form the surprise answer, as suggested by the above cartoon.

Print the SURPRISE ANSWER here

JUMBLE®

Unscramble these four Jumbles, one letter to each square, to form four ordinary words.

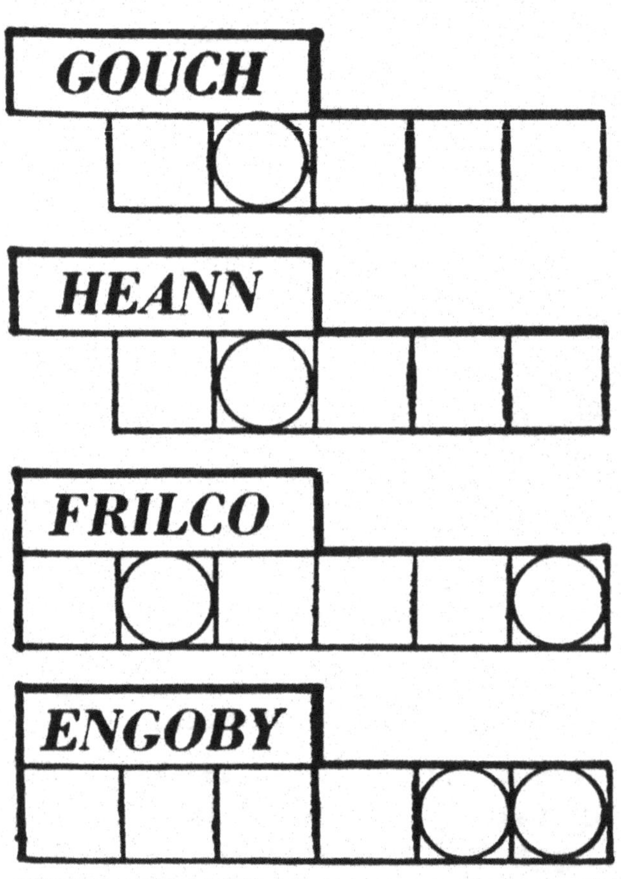
GOUCH
HEANN
FRILCO
ENGOBY
Print the SURPRISE ANSWER here

Again in France?

Now arrange the circled letters to form the surprise answer, as suggested by the above cartoon.

34

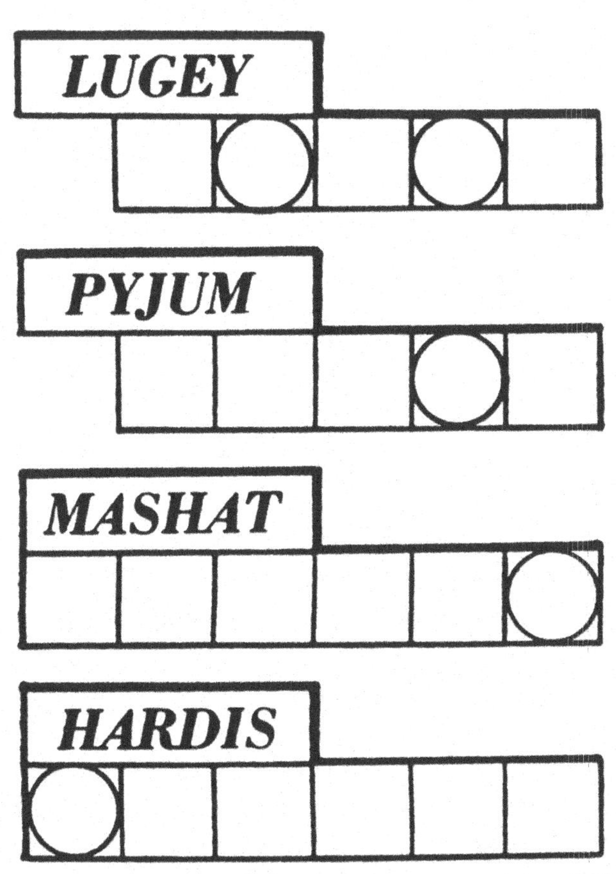

JUMBLE®

Unscramble these four Jumbles, one letter to each square, to form four ordinary words.

LUGEY

PYJUM

MASHAT

HARDIS

She's a gem and much rarer than the mother of her

Now arrange the circled letters to form the surprise answer, as suggested by the above cartoon.

Print the SURPRISE ANSWER here

35

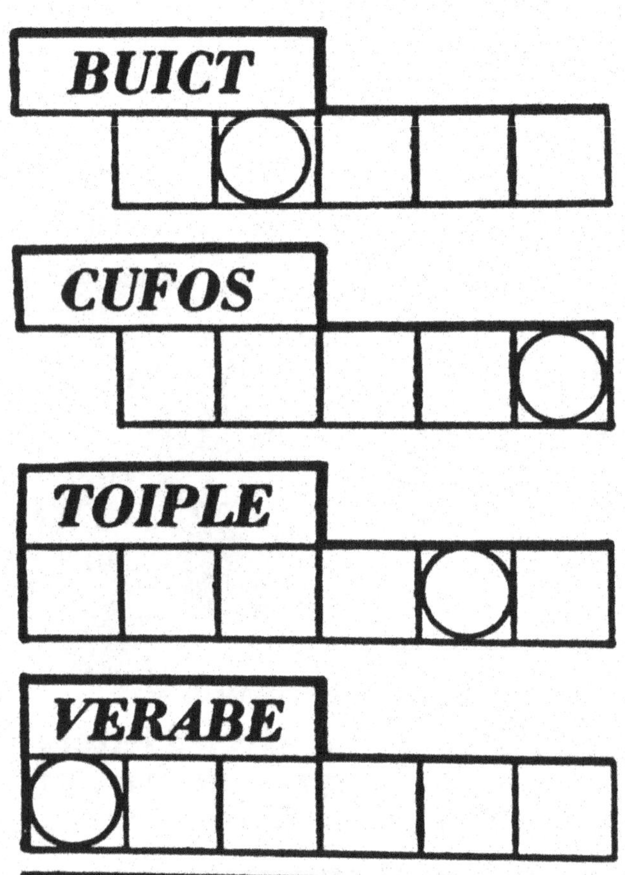
JUMBLE®
Unscramble these four Jumbles, one letter to each square, to form four ordinary words.
BUICT
CUFOS
TOIPLE
VERABE

I maintain...
On the contrary...
THERE MAY BE OBJECTIONS INVOLVED IN THE USE OF THESE WORDS!

Now arrange the circled letters to form the surprise answer, as suggested by the above cartoon.

Print the SURPRISE ANSWER here

36

JUMBLE®

Unscramble these four Jumbles, one letter to each square, to form four ordinary words.

NYOME

UNDOB

EMFONT

GANDIL

Come out in the garden!
How beautiful!

Now arrange the circled letters to form the surprise answer, as suggested by the above cartoon.

Print the SURPRISE ANSWER here

“ ”

JUMBLE®

Unscramble these four Jumbles, one letter to each square, to form four ordinary words.

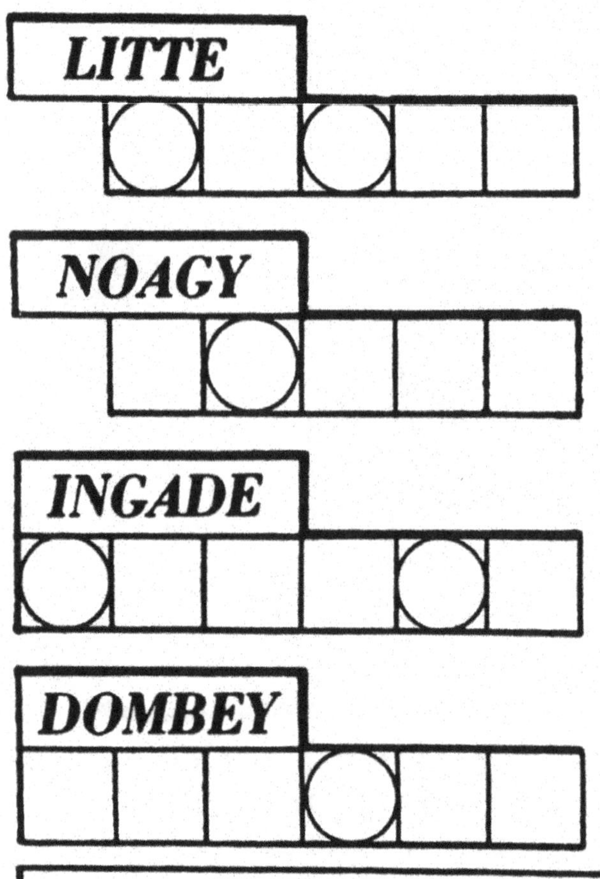
LITTE
NOAGY
INGADE
DOMBEY

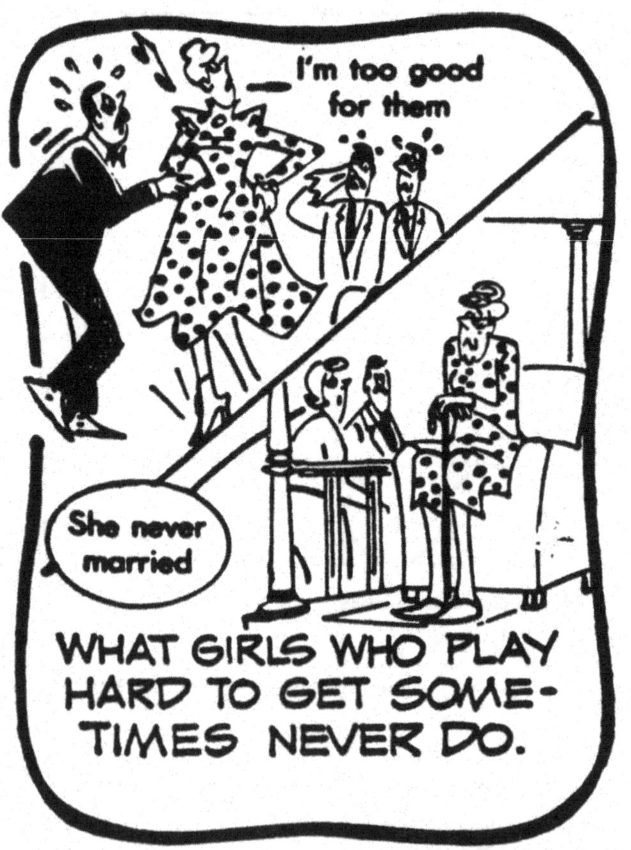
I'm too good for them
She never married
WHAT GIRLS WHO PLAY HARD TO GET SOMETIMES NEVER DO.

Now arrange the circled letters to form the surprise answer, as suggested by the above cartoon.

Print the SURPRISE ANSWER here

DAILY
JUMBLE®
Jubilee

38

JUMBLE®

Unscramble these four Jumbles, one letter to each square, to form four ordinary words.

LAVIA

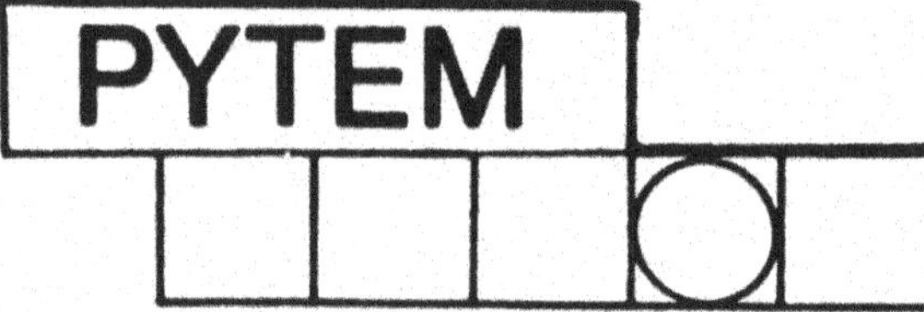
PYTEM

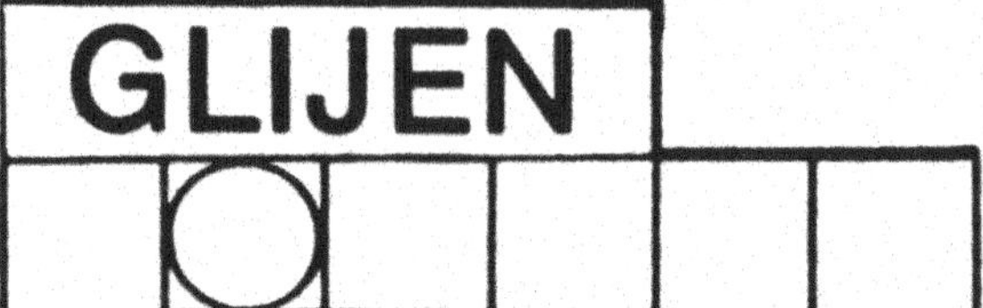
GLIJEN

EPSOOP

High-class party
COULD BE THE RESULT OF A TOSS-UP— WHAT YOU SHOULD WEAR.

Now arrange the circled letters to form the surprise answer, as suggested by the above cartoon.

Print answer here: ""

Unscramble these four Jumbles, one letter to each square, to form four ordinary words.

DUSEE

VOLEN

AMBALS

CLITIE

WHAT HOT MUSIC
DOES TO PEOPLE
WITH "SQUARE" TASTES.

Now arrange the circled letters to form the surprise answer, as suggested by the above cartoon.

Answer:  THEM 

40

JUMBLE®

Unscramble these four Jumbles, one letter to each square, to form four ordinary words.

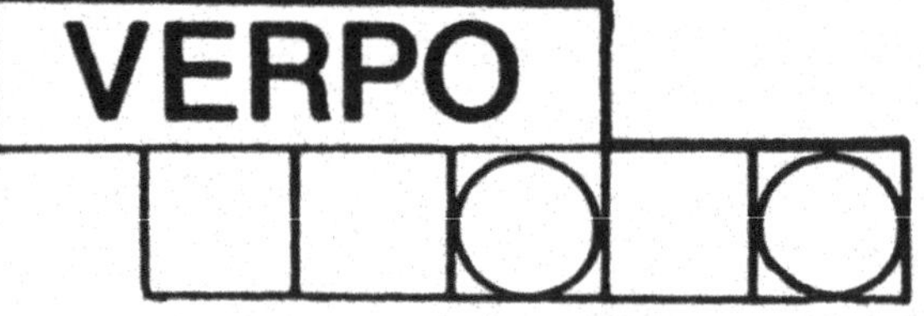
VERPO

YUSUR

TRAMPE

ROHORR

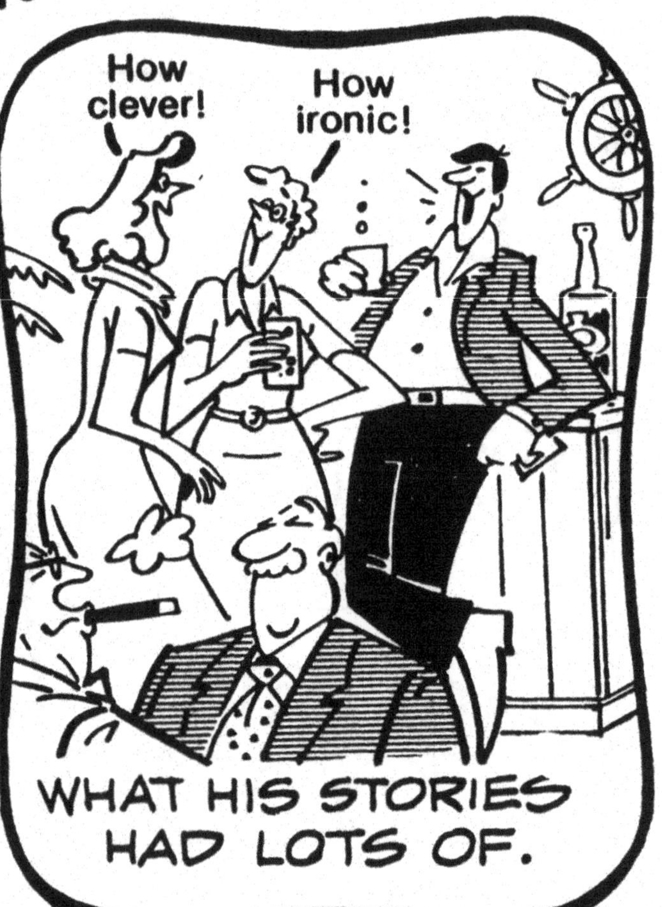
How clever!
How ironic!
WHAT HIS STORIES HAD LOTS OF.

Now arrange the circled letters to form the surprise answer, as suggested by the above cartoon.

Print answer here:  

41

JUMBLE®

Unscramble these four Jumbles, one letter to each square, to form four ordinary words.

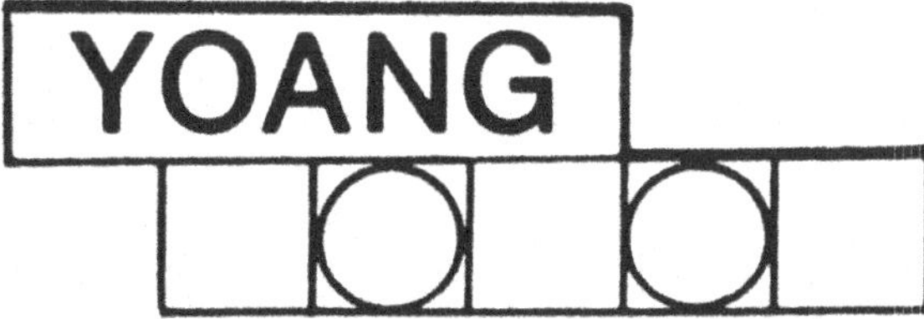
YOANG

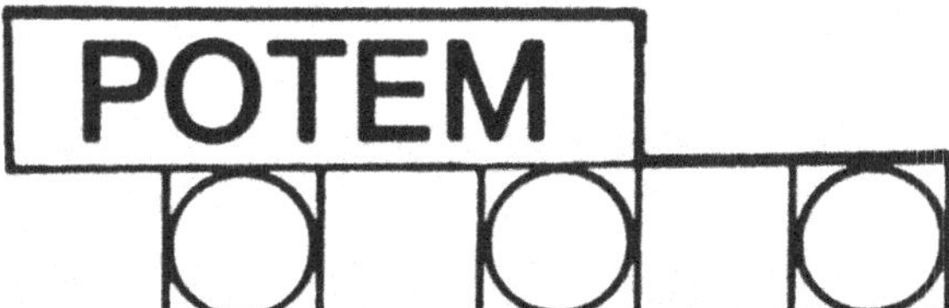
POTEM

VINNET

CAMIOT

WHAT THE TRUMPET PLAYER'S GIRL FRIEND ACCUSED HIM OF DOING.

Now arrange the circled letters to form the surprise answer, as suggested by the above cartoon.

Answer: ◯◯◯◯-◯◯◯◯◯◯ HER

JUMBLE®

Unscramble these four Jumbles, one letter to each square, to form four ordinary words.

YAHIR

DEVEL

SOXEEP

HOCCUR

"HERE'S HOW!"— IN THE KITCHEN.

Now arrange the circled letters to form the surprise answer, as suggested by the above cartoon.

Print answer here: 

JUMBLE®

Unscramble these four Jumbles, one letter to each square, to form four ordinary words.

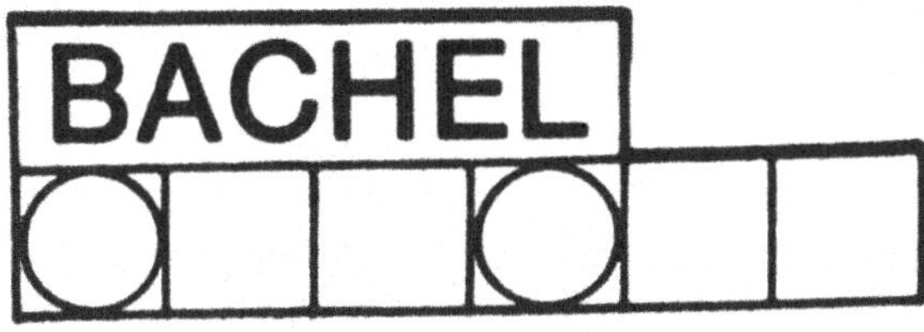

JOE'S
JOE'S
THIS RATHER UNCOUTH CHARACTER HAS A COUPLE OF BARS.

Now arrange the circled letters to form the surprise answer, as suggested by the above cartoon.

Answer here: A" ▢▢▢-▢▢▢-▢▢▢ "

44

JUMBLE®

Unscramble these four Jumbles, one letter to each square, to form four ordinary words.

LYMIF

OVEBA

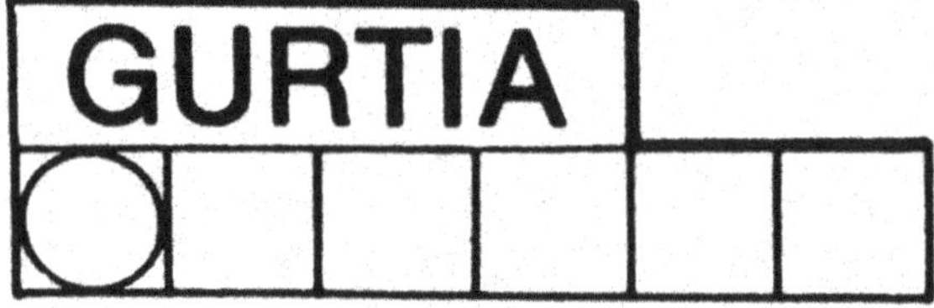
GURTIA

KONVIE

It's all his!
WHAT HE CAME INTO WHEN HE WAS BORN.

Now arrange the circled letters to form the surprise answer, as suggested by the above cartoon.

Print answer here: 

45

Unscramble these four Jumbles, one letter to each square, to form four ordinary words.

NOAKE

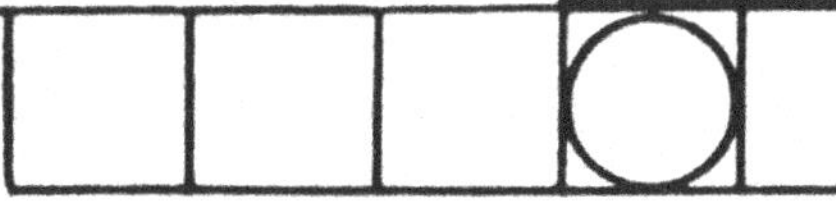

SHWIK

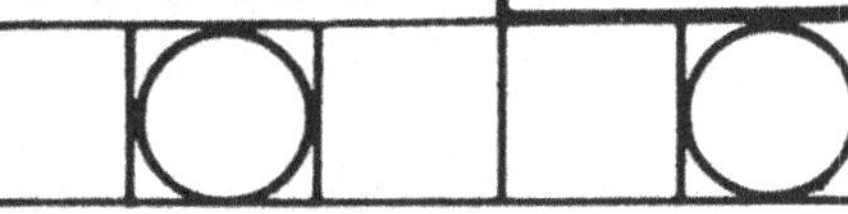

FLUTAR

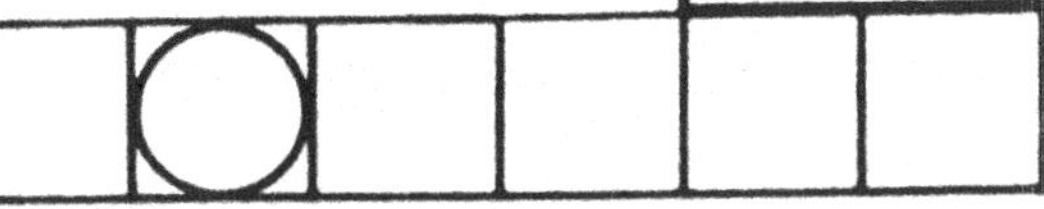

COSTAM

AGITATED WHERE COCKTAILS ARE CONCERNED.

Now arrange the circled letters to form the surprise answer, as suggested by the above cartoon.

Print answer here: THE 

46

JUMBLE®

Unscramble these four Jumbles, one letter to each square, to form four ordinary words.

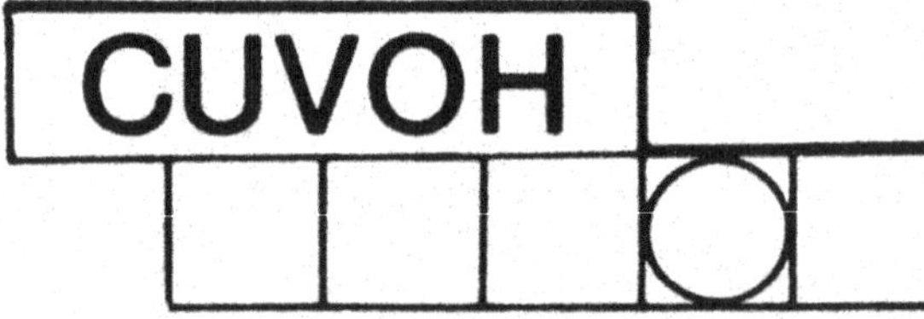
CUVOH

BLAWR

INREEM

ROCTAV

A BAD HABIT
MIGHT GET A
"GRIP" ON ONE.

Now arrange the circled letters to form the surprise answer, as suggested by the above cartoon.

Print answer here: 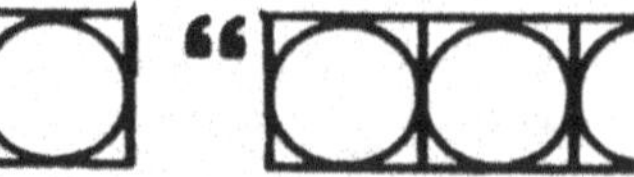

47

JUMBLE®

Unscramble these four Jumbles, one letter to each square, to form four ordinary words.

GURAU

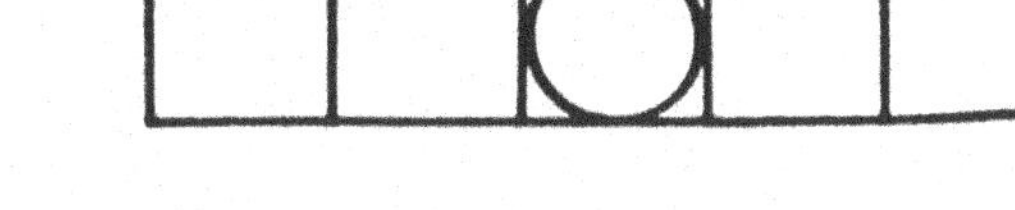

SHLYP

KLAYEC

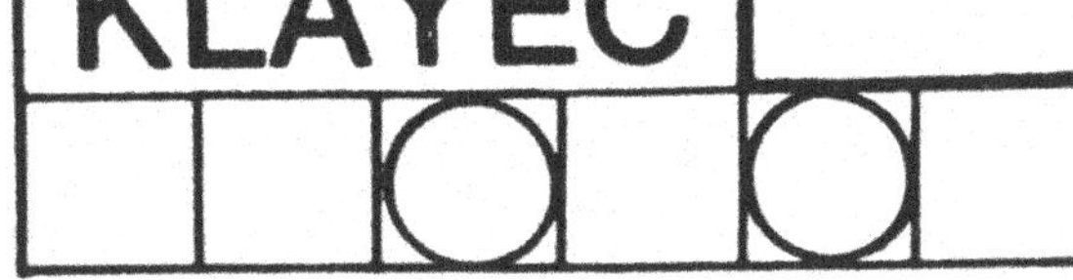

ZAHDAR

Rich widow
IT REQUIRES AN EFFORT OF WILL TO LEAVE IT.

Now arrange the circled letters to form the surprise answer, as suggested by the above cartoon.

Print answer here: A 

48

JUMBLE®

Unscramble these four Jumbles, one letter to each square, to form four ordinary words.

ORSAL

HOALT

TRIMOP

GLEENT

SOUNDS COMFORTABLY SICK.

Now arrange the circled letters to form the surprise answer, as suggested by the above cartoon.

Print answer here: " "

49

JUMBLE®

Unscramble these four Jumbles, one letter to each square, to form four ordinary words.

YAMOF

NIYKK

TURAIN

REOCAN

DOESN'T SOUND LIKE PREPARATION FOR WAR WHEN THEY ARM THUS.

Now arrange the circled letters to form the surprise answer, as suggested by the above cartoon.

Print answer here: "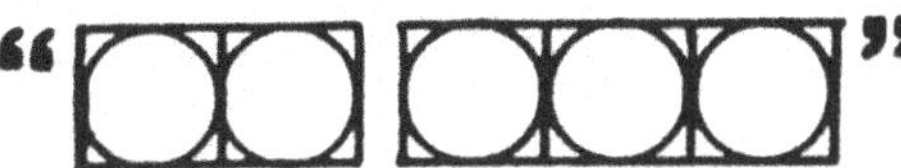"

50

JUMBLE®

Unscramble these four Jumbles, one letter to each square, to form four ordinary words.

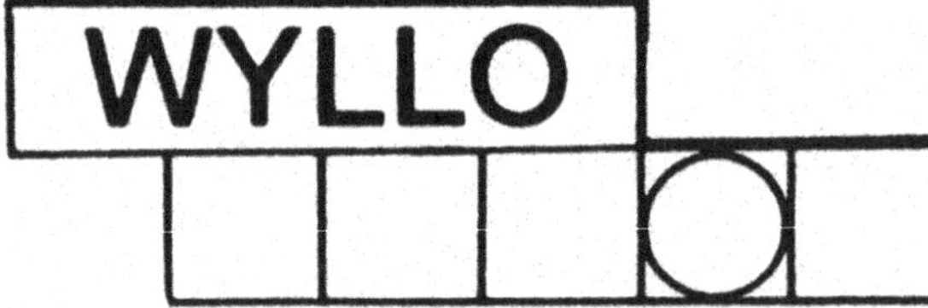
WYLLO

FASHE

LAYGEL

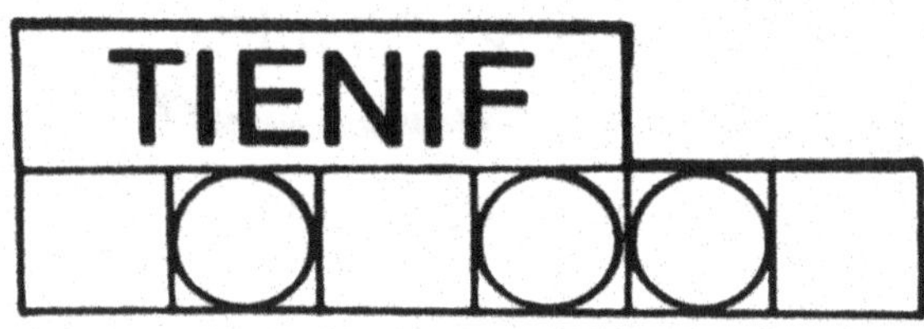
TIENIF

Revenooers!
A KIND OF "ART" YOU MIGHT BE SURPRISED TO FIND IN A MOVING PICTURE.

Now arrange the circled letters to form the surprise answer, as suggested by the above cartoon.

Answer here: "  " 

JUMBLE®

Unscramble these four Jumbles, one letter to each square, to form four ordinary words.

TEFAC

KULCC

OBNIBB

NYGERT

INCLINED TO BE ON THE THIN SIDE.

Now arrange the circled letters to form the surprise answer, as suggested by the above cartoon.

Print answer here: 

52

JUMBLE®

Unscramble these four Jumbles, one letter to each square, to form four ordinary words.

NUWDE

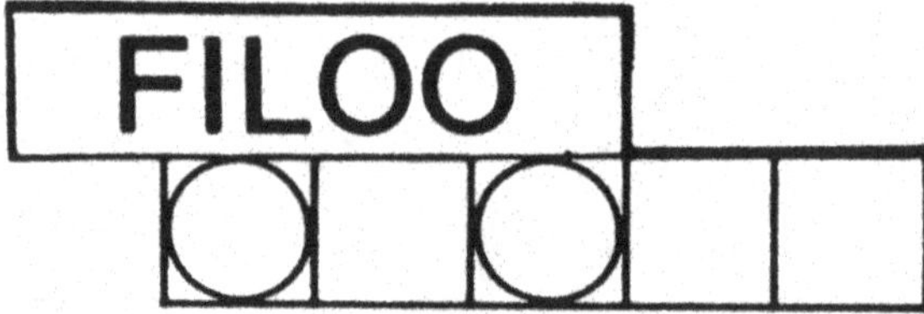

FILOO

RABLER

LURSEY

ND OPENING
BAR
Now we're in business!
IT WAS AWFUL— UNTIL A LETTER ARRIVED TO MAKE IT "LEGAL"!

Now arrange the circled letters to form the surprise answer, as suggested by the above cartoon.

Print answer here: 

53

JUMBLE®

Unscramble these four Jumbles, one letter to each square, to form four ordinary words.

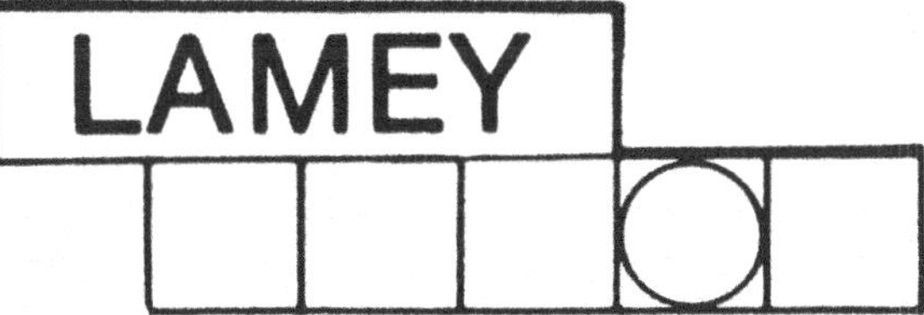
LAMEY

BICUT

ENBRAY

DESMOT

Too big a night?
OUT OF JAIL — AND ILL IN BED.

Now arrange the circled letters to form the surprise answer, as suggested by the above cartoon.

Print answer here:

54

JUMBLE®

Unscramble these four Jumbles, one letter to each square, to form four ordinary words.

YOCEV

GOBUM

TAWNUL

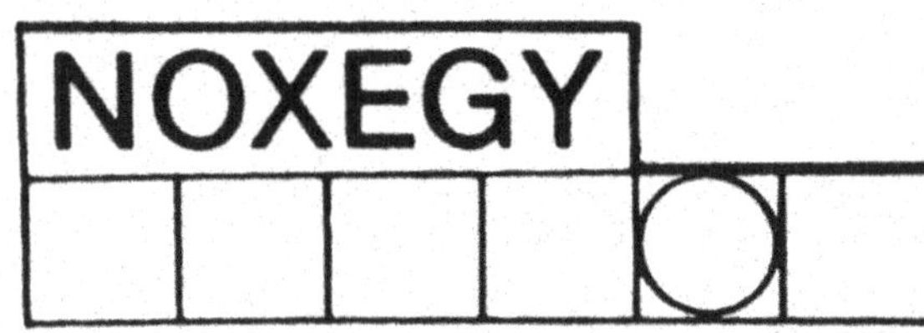

NOXEGY

How nice

THIS ROOM IS JUST RIGHT FOR COCKTAILS.

Now arrange the circled letters to form the surprise answer, as suggested by the above cartoon.

Print answer here: 

55

JUMBLE®

Unscramble these four Jumbles, one letter to each square, to form four ordinary words.

ELTAM

HOCAP

LEWVIE

NARLAC

JUST WHAT'S BEHIND SUCH PAINTING?

Now arrange the circled letters to form the surprise answer, as suggested by the above cartoon.

Print answer here: " "

56

JUMBLE®

Unscramble these four Jumbles, one letter to each square, to form four ordinary words.

VORLE

HORAB

LUFTAY

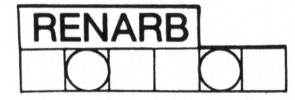

RENARB

WHAT THE FORTUNE-TELLER SAID WHEN ASKED HOW SHE FELT ABOUT HER WORK.

Now arrange the circled letters to form the surprise answer, as suggested by the above cartoon.

Print answer here: I  A

JUMBLE®

Unscramble these four Jumbles, one letter to each square, to form four ordinary words.

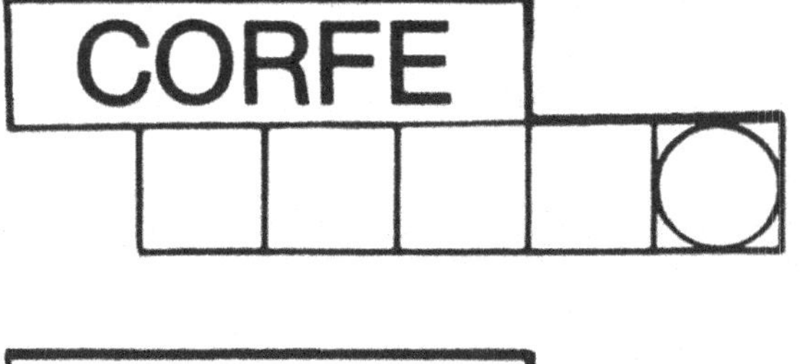
CORFE

PYMUB

DOLFUN

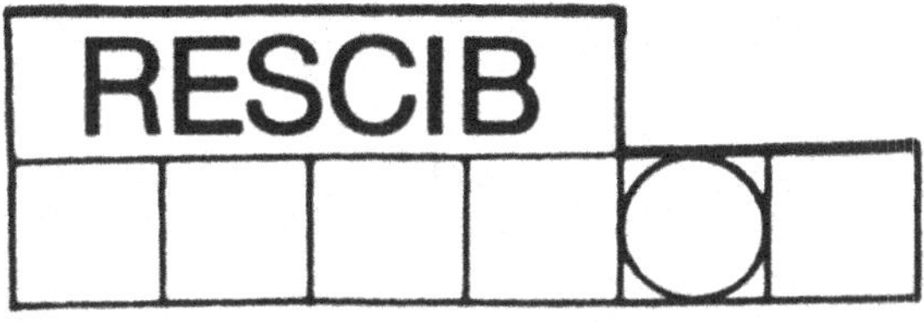
RESCIB

BOOM
WHAT THEY ALL GOT DURING A PARTY IN THE AIR RAID SHELTER.

Now arrange the circled letters to form the surprise answer, as suggested by the above cartoon.

Print answer here: “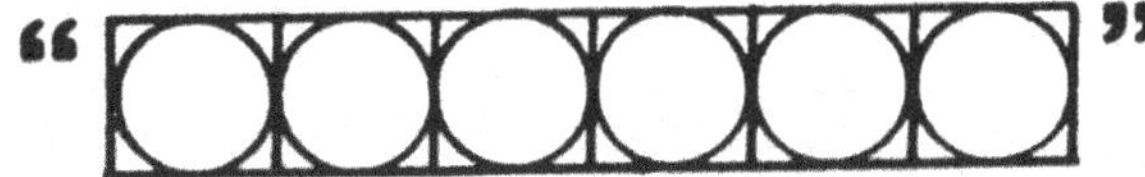”

Unscramble these four Jumbles, one letter to each square, to form four ordinary words.

ROLYG

DYSAN

FLUGEN

PREDIM

For a moment I thought he was losing his voice!

A SINGER "BREAKS DOWN" – BUT RECOVERS.

Now arrange the circled letters to form the surprise answer, as suggested by the above cartoon.

Print answer here: " "

59

JUMBLE®

Unscramble these four Jumbles, one letter to each square, to form four ordinary words.

ORRUJ

NAKEW

SYPORD

SHAUTI

STANDING ROOM ONLY
WHAT THE ARCHI-
TECT TURNED ACTOR
CERTAINLY KNEW
HOW TO DO.

Now arrange the circled letters to form the surprise answer, as suggested by the above cartoon.

Answer here:

60

JUMBLE®

Unscramble these four Jumbles, one letter to each square, to form four ordinary words.

TELAH

DEKEY

HINBED

UNISCO

"DISTURBED" THE SEDATE.

Now arrange the circled letters to form the surprise answer, as suggested by the above cartoon.

Print answer here: " "

JUMBLE®

Unscramble these four Jumbles, one letter to each square, to form four ordinary words.

NAWGO

SWYNE

RENITE

AUGIAN

WHAT THAT ATTRACTIVE LADY GAMBLER HAD.

Now arrange the circled letters to form the surprise answer, as suggested by the above cartoon.

Answer:

JUMBLE®

Unscramble these four Jumbles, one letter to each square, to form four ordinary words.

KLANE

OONES

GIRLYS

PREEMA

CAKE ONE MIGHT ENJOY WHILE TAKING A BATH.

Now arrange the circled letters to form the surprise answer, as suggested by the above cartoon.

Print answer here:

63

JUMBLE®

Unscramble these four Jumbles, one letter to each square, to form four ordinary words.

YUINT

TOABB

SOOPPE

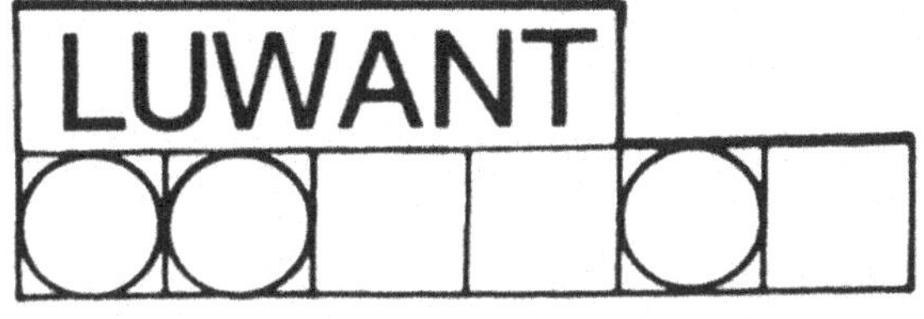
LUWANT

THE KING DECIDED TO HAVE SEVERAL COURT JESTERS SO HE COULD KEEP THIS.

Now arrange the circled letters to form the surprise answer, as suggested by the above cartoon.

Answer: HIS   HIM

64

JUMBLE®

Unscramble these four Jumbles, one letter to each square, to form four ordinary words.

VINEL

SILAA

DARWIN

TERVID

SHE'S AN ENTHUSI-
ASTIC PRIMA DONNA,
WHICHEVER WAY
YOU LOOK AT IT.

Now arrange the circled letters to form the surprise answer, as suggested by the above cartoon.

Print answer here: AN 

65

JUMBLE®

Unscramble these four Jumbles, one letter to each square, to form four ordinary words.

GLIBE

TOMIF

TINOOL

INSHIF

He's had too much
HOW PEOPLE WHO LIVE "LOOSE" LIVES SOMETIMES END UP.

Now arrange the circled letters to form the surprise answer, as suggested by the above cartoon.

Print answer here:

JUMBLE®

Unscramble these four Jumbles, one letter to each square, to form four ordinary words.

RICLY

GNUST

BOEDUL

SPEGOL

WHAT THE PRISONER WHO MADE MUSIC IN HIS CELL MUST HAVE BEEN.

Now arrange the circled letters to form the surprise answer, as suggested by the above cartoon.

Print answer here: A "◯◯◯◯-◯◯◯"

67

JUMBLE®

Unscramble these four Jumbles, one letter to each square, to form four ordinary words.

COTIN

LOFAR

SEIBED

MINOOT

MIGHT GO TO THE HEAD AT A STAG PARTY.

Now arrange the circled letters to form the surprise answer, as suggested by the above cartoon.

Print answer here:

68

JUMBLE®

Unscramble these four Jumbles, one letter to each square, to form four ordinary words.

LAURR

CAULD

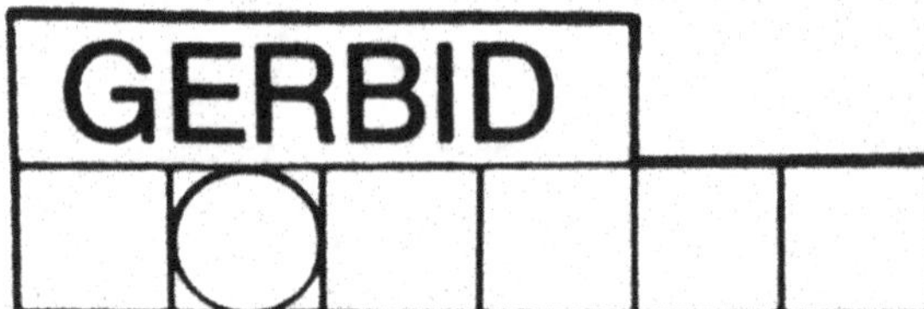
GERBID

TIPMER

WHAT PURE ART
CAN PRODUCE.

Now arrange the circled letters to form the surprise answer, as suggested by the above cartoon.

Print answer here: “”

JUMBLE®

Unscramble these four Jumbles, one letter to each square, to form four ordinary words.

DIMIO

BYRDE

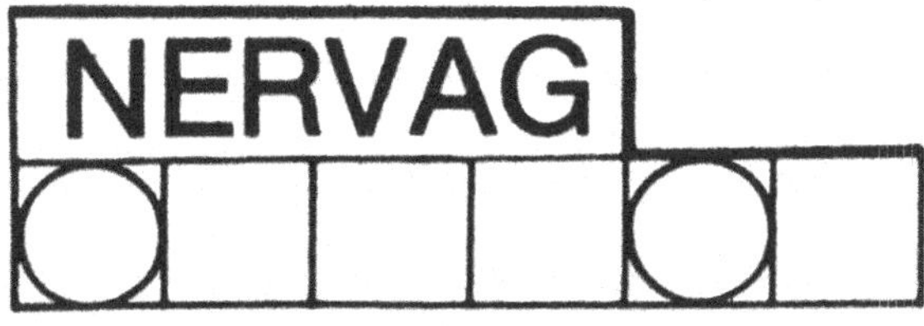
NERVAG

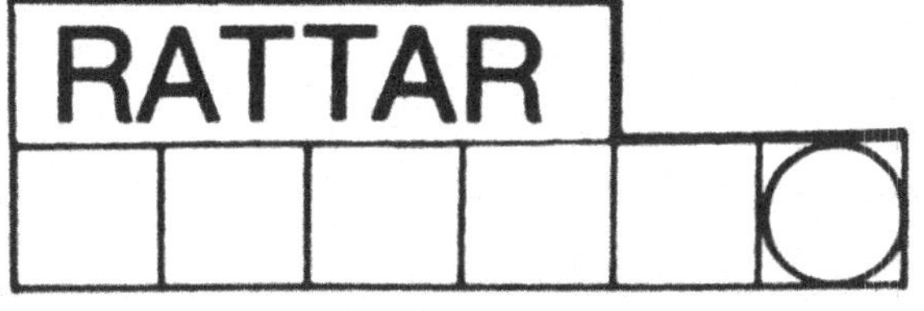
RATTAR

How about joining us in a little penny ante, Skipper?
THE CARD GAME THE CAPTAIN SHOULD STICK TO.

Now arrange the circled letters to form the surprise answer, as suggested by the above cartoon.

Print answer here: "  "

70

JUMBLE®

Unscramble these four Jumbles, one letter to each square, to form four ordinary words.

GITHE

PITED

SIBOPH

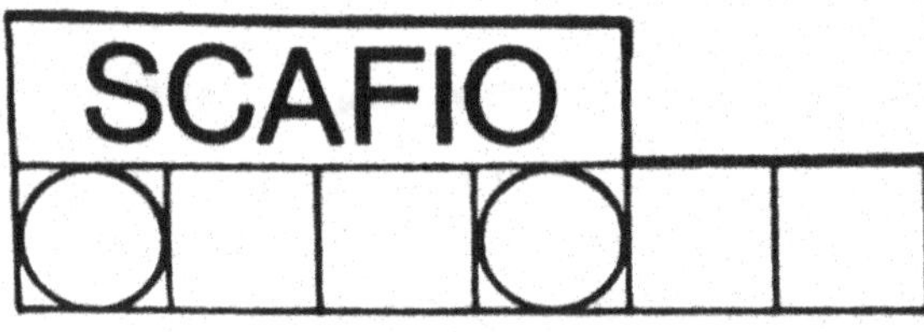
SCAFIO

Sorry, I've had too much to drink

Guess I'm tired

TWO THINGS THAT KEPT HIM FROM BEING A GOOD DANCER.

Now arrange the circled letters to form the surprise answer, as suggested by the above cartoon.

Print answer here:

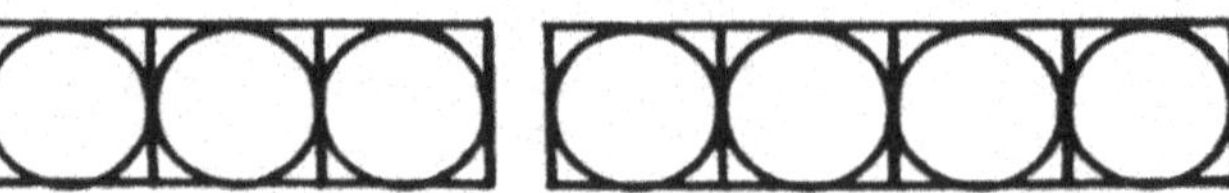

JUMBLE®

Unscramble these four Jumbles, one letter to each square, to form four ordinary words.

TIBUL

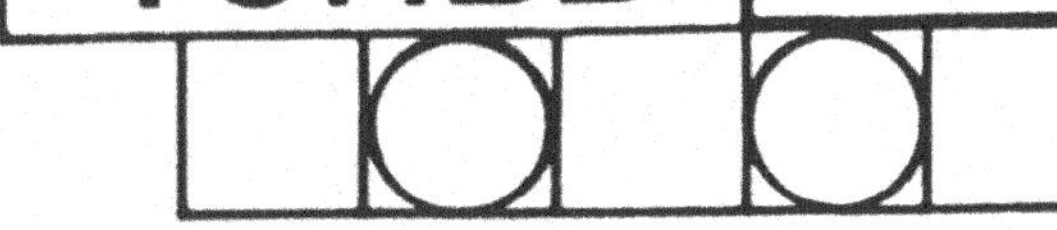

YOHBB

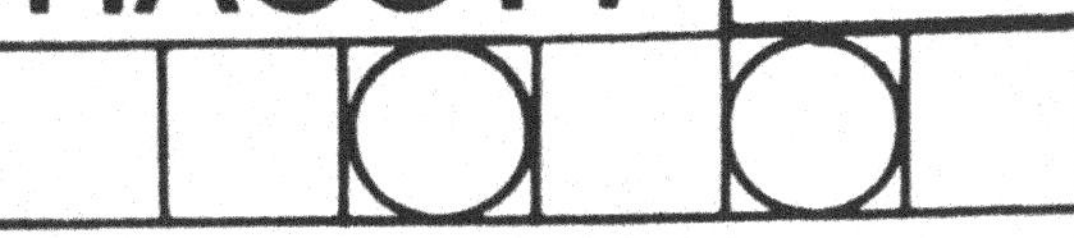

HACCYT

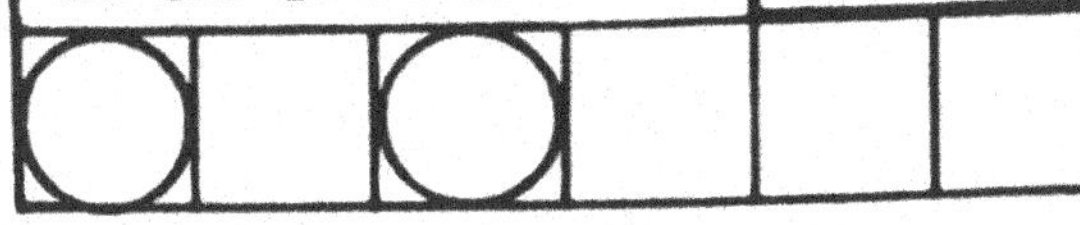

BLOMAG

Oops!
OFTEN OPENED BY MISTAKE.

Now arrange the circled letters to form the surprise answer, as suggested by the above cartoon.

Print answer here: A  

72

JUMBLE®

Unscramble these four Jumbles, one letter to each square, to form four ordinary words.

ROMAR

UNGLE

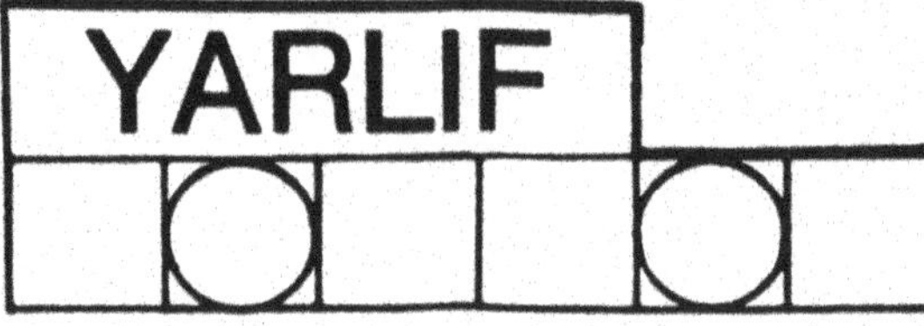

YARLIF

BOUSTE

Have another!
FREQUENTLY KEEP PEOPLE UNDER THE WEATHER.

Now arrange the circled letters to form the surprise answer, as suggested by the above cartoon.

Print answer here: 

JUMBLE®

Unscramble these four Jumbles, one letter to each square, to form four ordinary words.

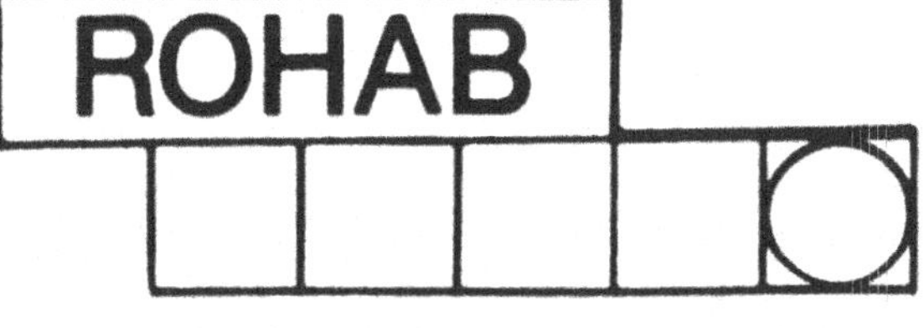
ROHAB

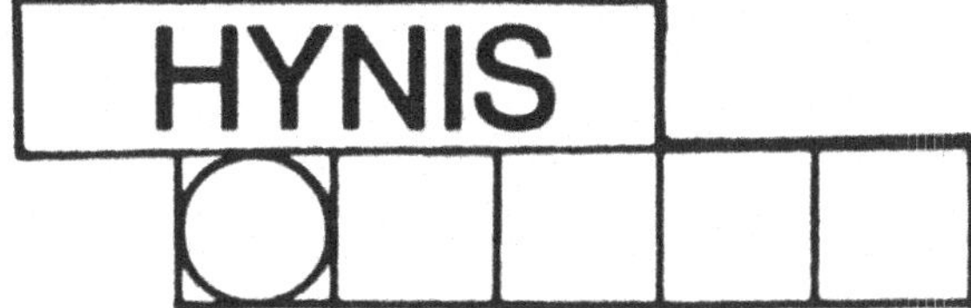
HYNIS

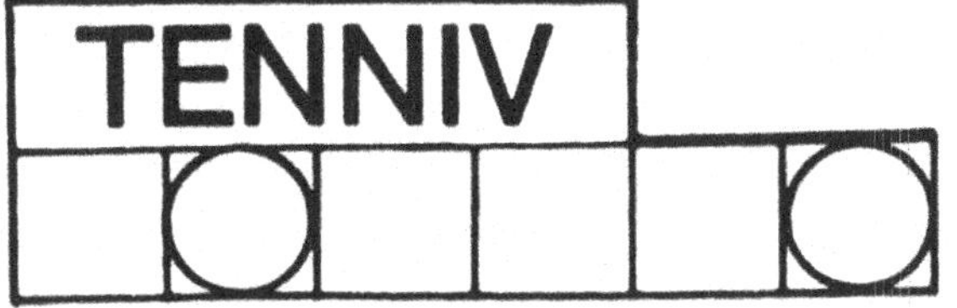
TENNIV

CIRPAY

Wow! That took some doing!
A TYPE OF MELODY EVIDENTLY REQUIRING CONSID-ERABLE EFFORT.

Now arrange the circled letters to form the surprise answer, as suggested by the above cartoon.

Print answer here: "  "

74

JUMBLE®

Unscramble these four Jumbles, one letter to each square, to form four ordinary words.

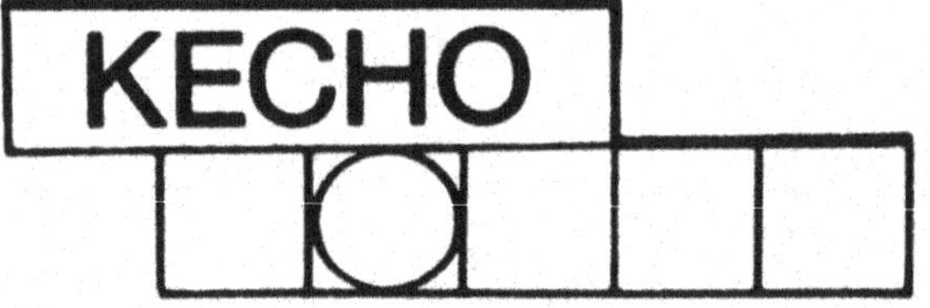
KECHO

POSOW

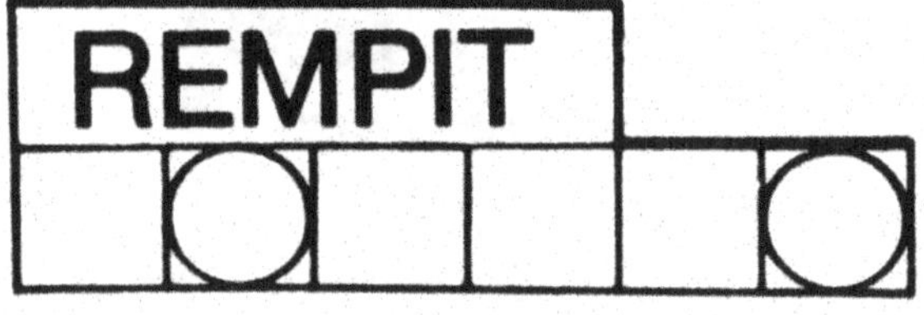
REMPIT

ENGOUT

You've had enough!

WHAT A MAN WHO DRINKS TO FORGET OFTEN FORGETS.

Now arrange the circled letters to form the surprise answer, as suggested by the above cartoon.

Print answer here:  TO 

75

JUMBLE®

Unscramble these four Jumbles, one letter to each square, to form four ordinary words.

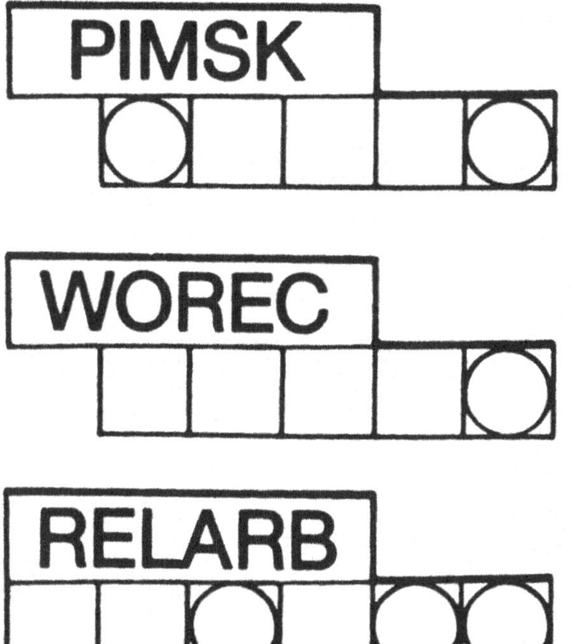
PIMSK
WOREC
RELARB

TALNED

WHAT THE BARTENDER WHO POURED THOSE EXTRA BIG DRINKS WAS KNOWN AS.

Now arrange the circled letters to form the surprise answer, as suggested by the above cartoon.

Answer: THE "   "

76

JUMBLE®

Unscramble these four Jumbles, one letter to each square, to form four ordinary words.

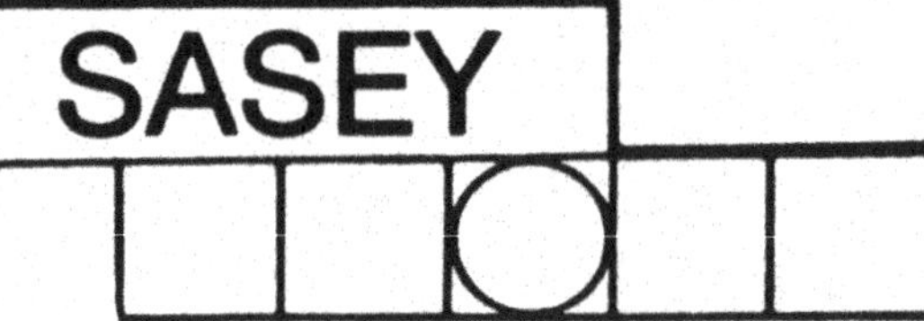
SASEY

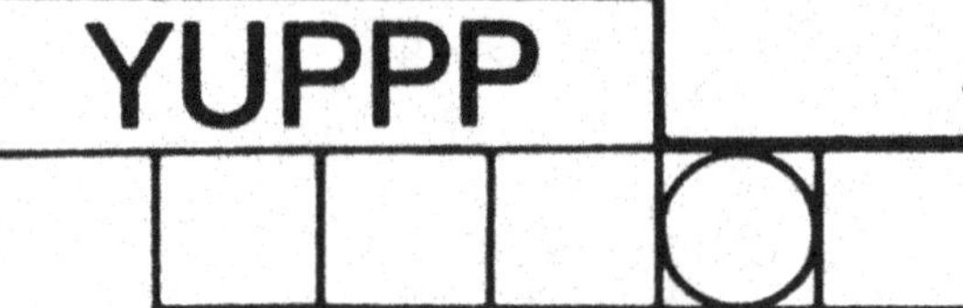
YUPPP

TRAFOC

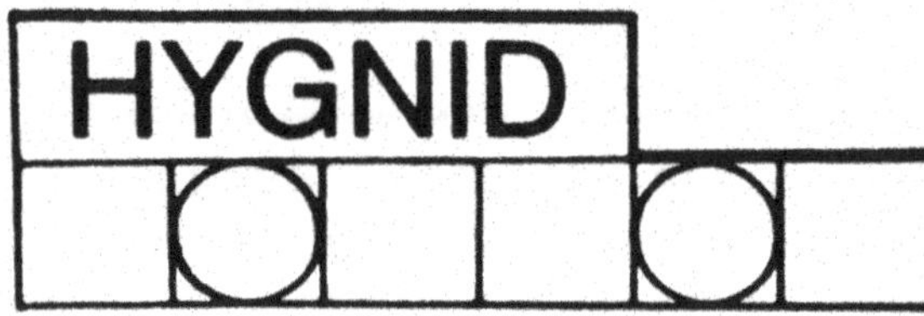
HYGNID

T-W-A-N-G

THIS PLAYER "BOTCHED" HIS PART.

Now arrange the circled letters to form the surprise answer, as suggested by the above cartoon.

Print answer here: ""

Unscramble these four Jumbles, one letter to each square, to form four ordinary words.

UNSEE

LAFAT

RANCOB

SURJIT

JOE'S
GRILL
CAFE
HE TRIED TO COMPOSE A DRINKING SONG BUT DIDN'T MAKE IT PAST THIS.

Now arrange the circled letters to form the surprise answer, as suggested by the above cartoon.

Answer: THE ◯◯◯◯◯ 2 ◯◯◯◯

78

JUMBLE®

Unscramble these four Jumbles, one letter to each square, to form four ordinary words.

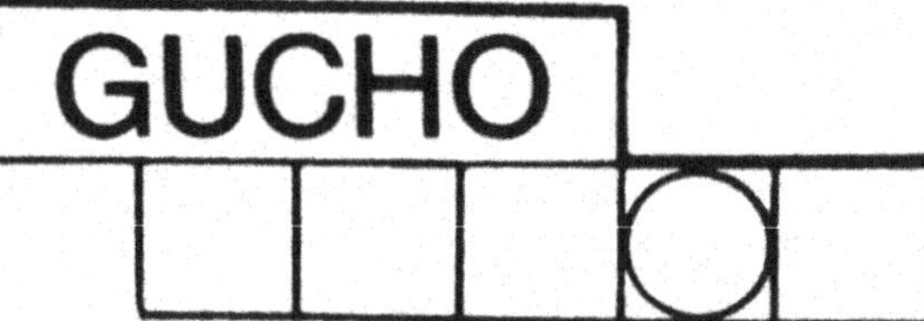
GUCHO

RATIE

UNTAUM

DILFED

CONCERT TON
WHAT TIME IS IT
WHEN CLOTHES
WEAR OUT?

Now arrange the circled letters to form the surprise answer, as suggested by the above cartoon.

Print answer here:

JUMBLE®

Unscramble these four Jumbles, one letter to each square, to form four ordinary words.

PHOWO

ICHED

MUNCOL

NIXFIG

LANGUAGE USED BY THOSE PRETENTIOUS JET-SETTERS.

Now arrange the circled letters to form the surprise answer, as suggested by the above cartoon.

Answer here: 

JUMBLE®

Unscramble these four Jumbles, one letter to each square, to form four ordinary words.

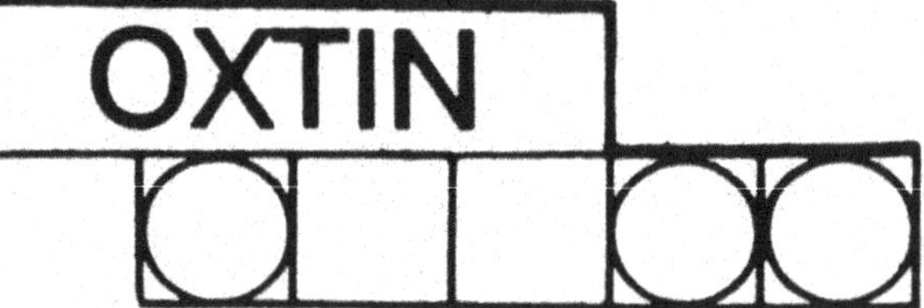
OXTIN

SINUM

HARANG

INGRIF

YE
OLDE

WHAT THOSE BOXERS ENGAGED IN WHILE HAVING A FEW DRINKS.

Now arrange the circled letters to form the surprise answer, as suggested by the above cartoon.

Answer: " ◯◯◯ " ◯◯◯◯◯◯◯◯

81

JUMBLE®

Unscramble these four Jumbles, one letter to each square, to form four ordinary words.

SEHCS

NUWDE

YERSIM

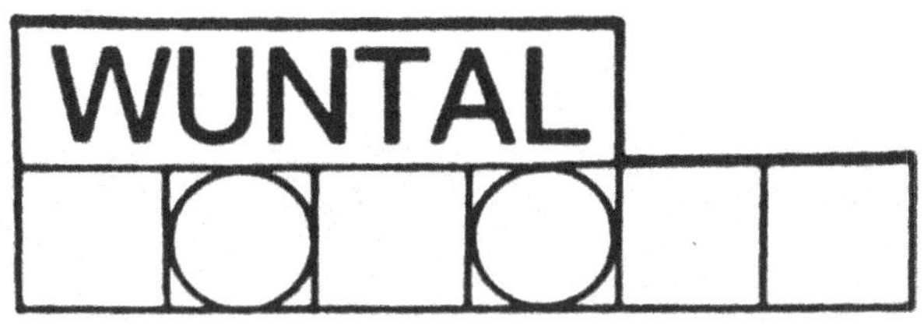
WUNTAL

SHE ADMITTED SHE WAS FORTY BUT SHE DIDN'T DO THIS.

Now arrange the circled letters to form the surprise answer, as suggested by the above cartoon.

Print answer here:

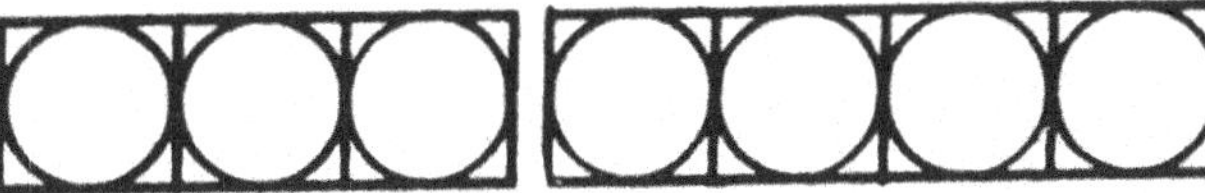

82

JUMBLE®

Unscramble these four Jumbles, one letter to each square, to form four ordinary words.

EMICH

UGGEA

CUNBOE

FLOAWL

SOME PEOPLE WHO THINK THEY'RE VERY FUNNY ARE REALLY JUST THIS.

Now arrange the circled letters to form the surprise answer, as suggested by the above cartoon.

Print answer here: 

83

JUMBLE®

Unscramble these four Jumbles, one letter to each square, to form four ordinary words.

TUNYT

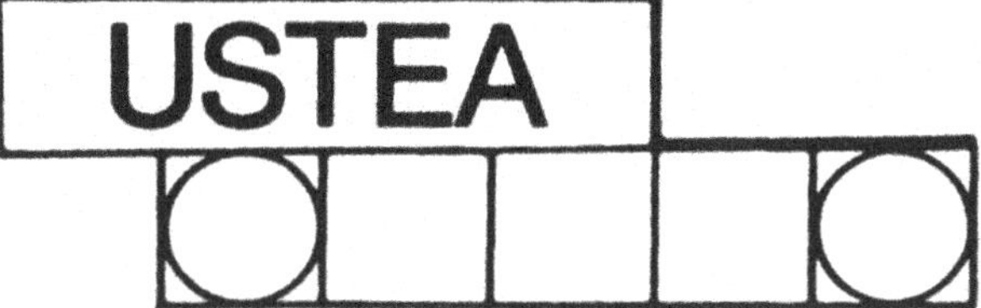
USTEA

LACKAJ

TOORRA

WHAT THEY TOLD AT THE FOOT DOCTORS' ANNUAL SHINDIG.

Now arrange the circled letters to form the surprise answer, as suggested by the above cartoon.

Answer: " ◯◯◯◯◯ " ◯◯◯◯◯

84

JUMBLE®

Unscramble these four Jumbles, one letter to each square, to form four ordinary words.

LAWRB

PUDMY

DAHLER

GLAARN

HONK!
WHAT IT MIGHT BE WHEN YOU GAMBOL ACROSS THE STREET.

Now arrange the circled letters to form the surprise answer, as suggested by the above cartoon.

Print answer here:

85

JUMBLE®

Unscramble these four Jumbles, one letter to each square, to form four ordinary words.

POKAK

ISTOC

LOORIE

YOUTCH

A COWBOY WHO TALKS FIRST AND THINKS AFTERWARDS MIGHT DO THIS.

Now arrange the circled letters to form the surprise answer, as suggested by the above cartoon.

Answer:  FROM THE 

86

JUMBLE®

Unscramble these four Jumbles, one letter to each square, to form four ordinary words.

DYKEE

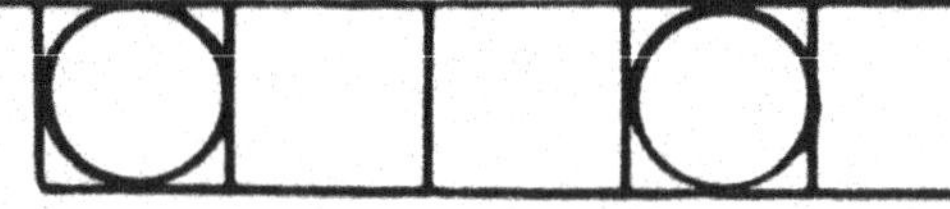

CIROU

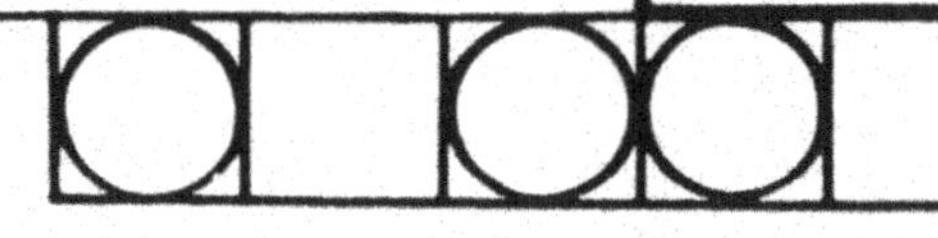
RYVETS

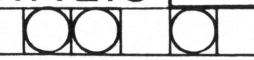

WALCOL

He's a scream!
WHAT YOU CAN EXPECT A SMART COOKIE TO BE.

Now arrange the circled letters to form the surprise answer, as suggested by the above cartoon.

Answer: A  "  "

87

JUMBLE®

Unscramble these four Jumbles, one letter to each square, to form four ordinary words.

TARAP

CAPHO

POAFFY

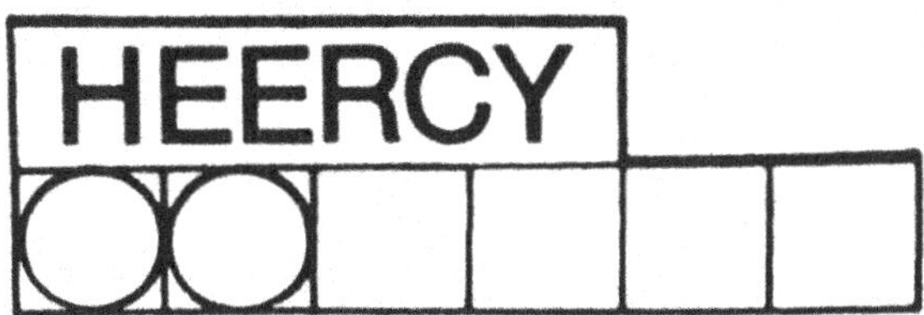

HEERCY

WHAT THEY CALLED THE POLICE OFFICERS' ANNUAL SHINDIG.

Now arrange the circled letters to form the surprise answer, as suggested by the above cartoon.

Print answer here: THE ""

88

JUMBLE®

Unscramble these four Jumbles, one letter to each square, to form four ordinary words.

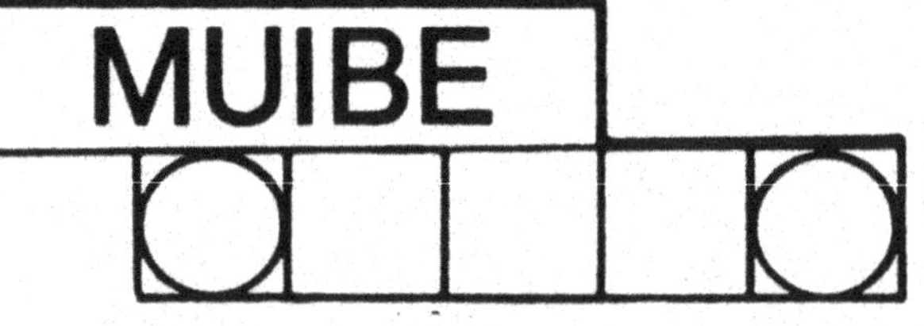

MUIBE

SULLK

DACLUN

MYSLOB

CONCER
TONITE
WHAT THE GUY WHOSE SHOES SQUEAKED MUST HAVE HAD.

Now arrange the circled letters to form the surprise answer, as suggested by the above cartoon.

Answer: ◯◯◯◯◯ IN HIS "◯◯◯◯"

89

JUMBLE®

Unscramble these four Jumbles, one letter to each square, to form four ordinary words.

TYJET

YARIN

RODIAT

VEELAC

WHAT THE BALLERINA INSISTED THAT HER PARTNER DO.

Now arrange the circled letters to form the surprise answer, as suggested by the above cartoon.

Answer here: "  " THE 

90

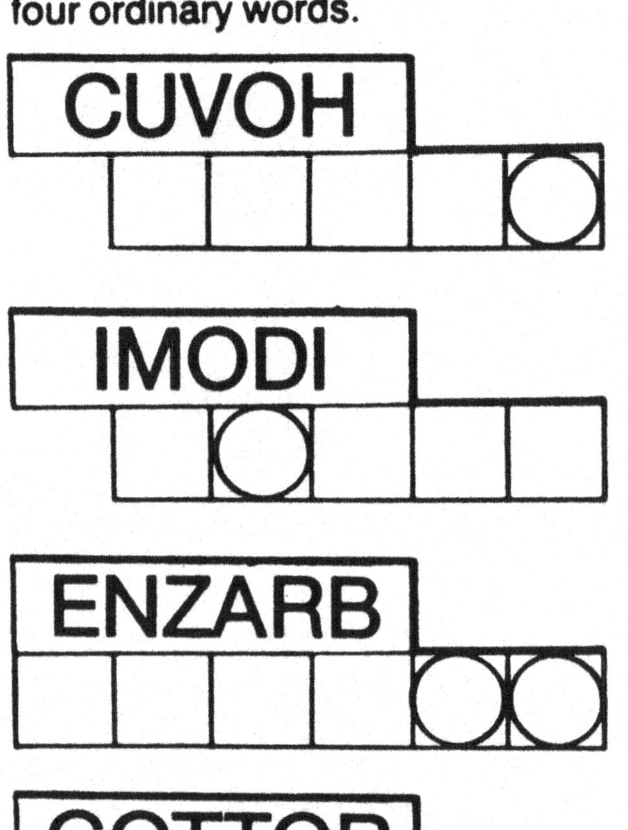
JUMBLE®
CUVOH
IMODI
ENZARB

Unscramble these four Jumbles, one letter to each square, to form four ordinary words.

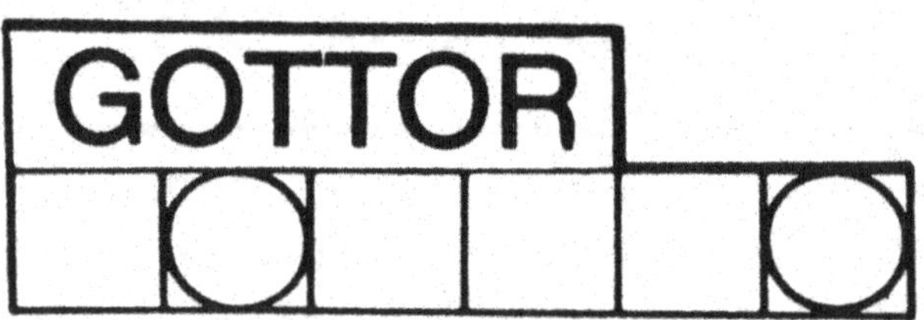
GOTTOR

Who invited HIM?

HOW DID THE TRUMPET PLAYER MANAGE TO GET INTO THAT EXCLUSIVE PARTY?

Now arrange the circled letters to form the surprise answer, as suggested by the above cartoon.

Print answer here: HE "  " IN

91

JUMBLE®

Unscramble these four Jumbles, one letter to each square, to form four ordinary words.

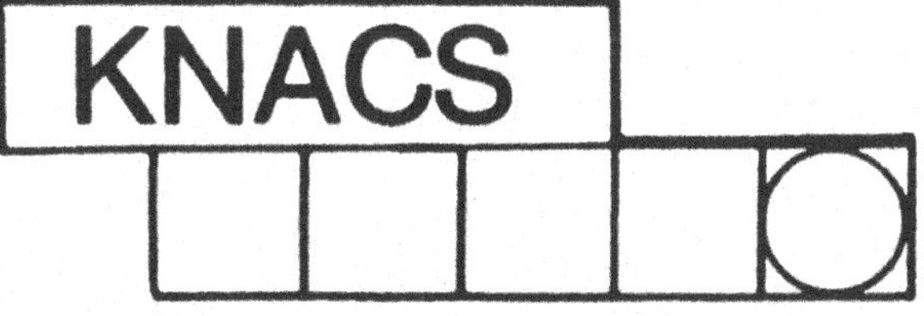
KNACS

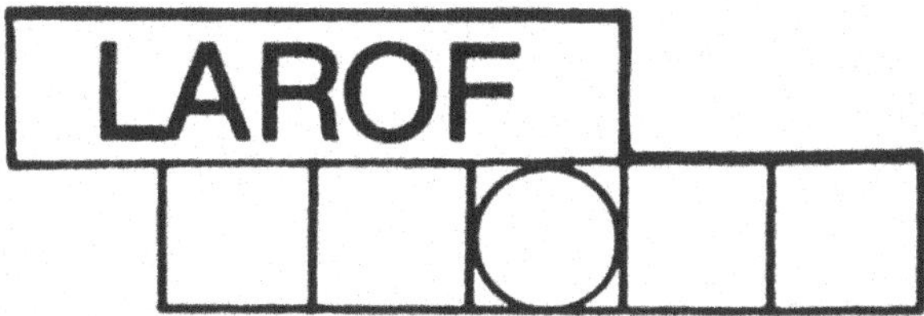
LAROF

LUGGEJ

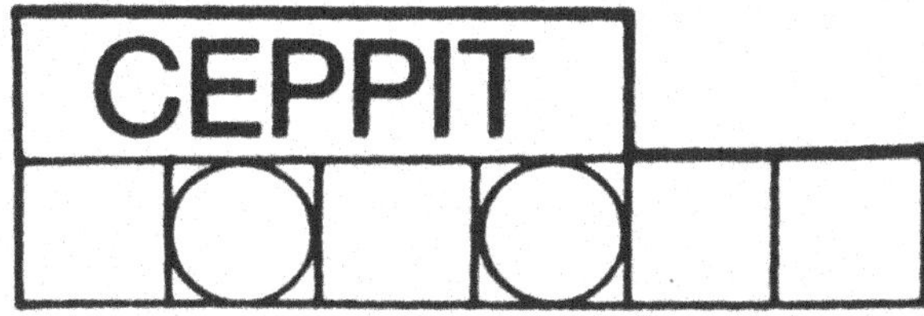
CEPPIT

WHAT HE WHO
LAUGHS LAST OFTEN
DOESN'T DO.

Now arrange the circled letters to form the surprise answer, as suggested by the above cartoon.

Print answer here:  THE 

92

JUMBLE®

Unscramble these four Jumbles, one letter to each square, to form four ordinary words.

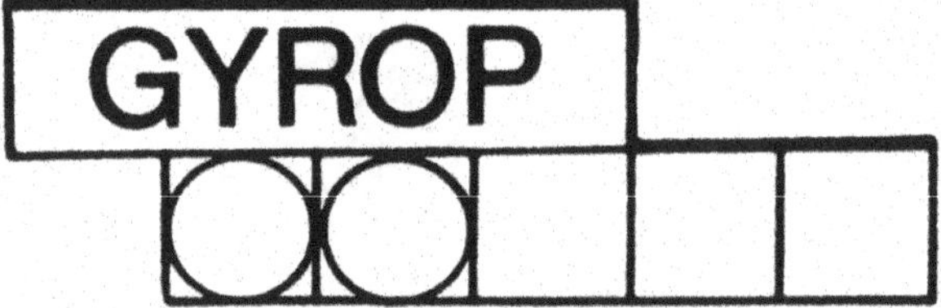
GYROP

RARIF

ROHORR

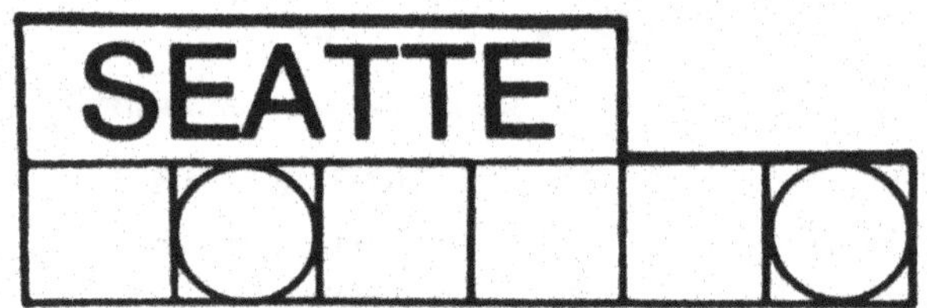
SEATTE

DID YOU HEAR MY LAST JOKE?

Now arrange the circled letters to form the surprise answer, as suggested by the above cartoon.

Print answer here: "   "

93

JUMBLE®

Unscramble these four Jumbles, one letter to each square, to form four ordinary words.

ROHTT

ILFOO

GIANAU

UMLUTT

Won't he ever forget it?!

THE IMPRESSION MADE ON ONE WHO'S BEEN IN THE NAVY MIGHT BE QUITE LASTING.

Now arrange the circled letters to form the surprise answer, as suggested by the above cartoon.

Print answer here:

94

JUMBLE®

Unscramble these four Jumbles, one letter to each square, to form four ordinary words.

TILOP

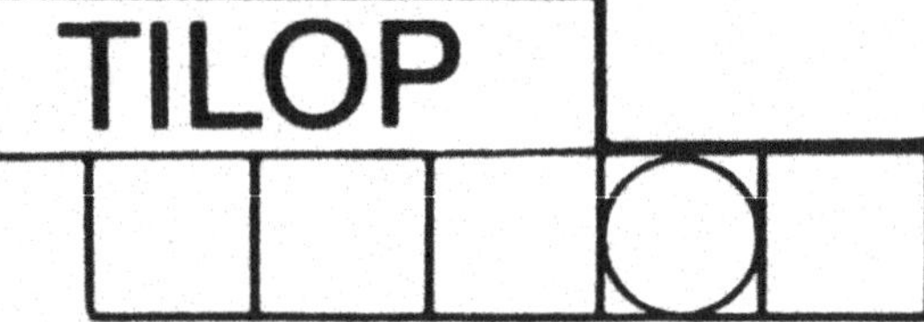

GACIM

RECUPS

CUNESS

He's always insulting people!
YOU'D GET NO PRAISES FROM THIS.

Now arrange the circled letters to form the surprise answer, as suggested by the above cartoon.

Answer: AN "◯◯◯◯◯◯◯◯◯"

95

JUMBLE®

Unscramble these four Jumbles, one letter to each square, to form four ordinary words.

OEGOS

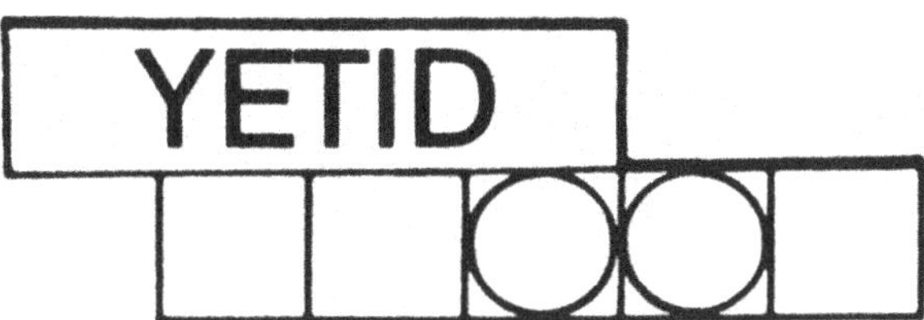
YETID

CHINLE

TINVER

Addio
MUCH OF THE AUDIENCE AT THAT OPERA HOUSE WAS THIS.

Now arrange the circled letters to form the surprise answer, as suggested by the above cartoon.

Print answer here:

96

JUMBLE®

Unscramble these four Jumbles, one letter to each square, to form four ordinary words.

LEKAN

KECAD

RETINE

SURDIA

This is getting monotonous
WHAT A VERY REPETITIVE TYPE OF DANCE MIGHT BE CALLED.

Now arrange the circled letters to form the surprise answer, as suggested by the above cartoon.

Answer: A " ☐☐☐☐☐ - ☐☐☐☐☐ "

JUMBLE®

Unscramble these four Jumbles, one letter to each square, to form four ordinary words.

CEKOH

GURPE

RANCLE

MUBHEL

Have you decided yet where we're going?
SOMETHING A WOMAN FINDS EASIER TO DO WITH HER FACE THAN WITH HER MIND.

Now arrange the circled letters to form the surprise answer, as suggested by the above cartoon.

Print answer here:  

98

JUMBLE®

Unscramble these four Jumbles, one letter to each square, to form four ordinary words.

UGSIE

SAYES

MEENAC

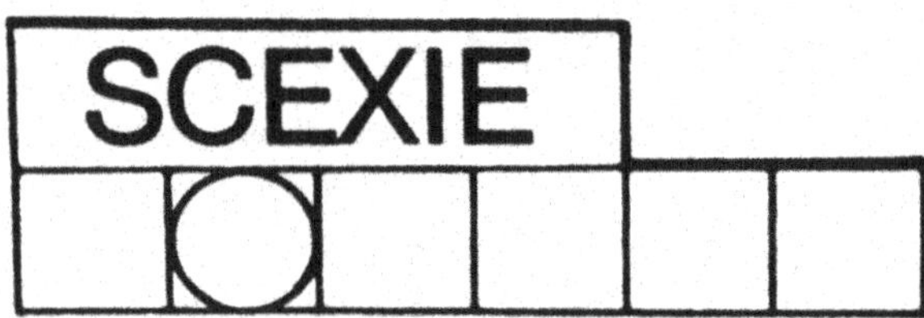
SCEXIE

To our beloved boss!
WHAT SOME PEOPLE ENJOY DRINKING TO.

Now arrange the circled letters to form the surprise answer, as suggested by the above cartoon.

Print answer here: 

99

JUMBLE®

Unscramble these four Jumbles, one letter to each square, to form four ordinary words.

DRUGO

HERIK

BOINAL

WOBELL

WHAT THEY SAID ABOUT THAT EVENING GOWN.

Now arrange the circled letters to form the surprise answer, as suggested by the above cartoon.

Answer: "☐☐☐! — & ☐☐☐☐☐☐"

100

JUMBLE®

Unscramble these four Jumbles, one letter to each square, to form four ordinary words.

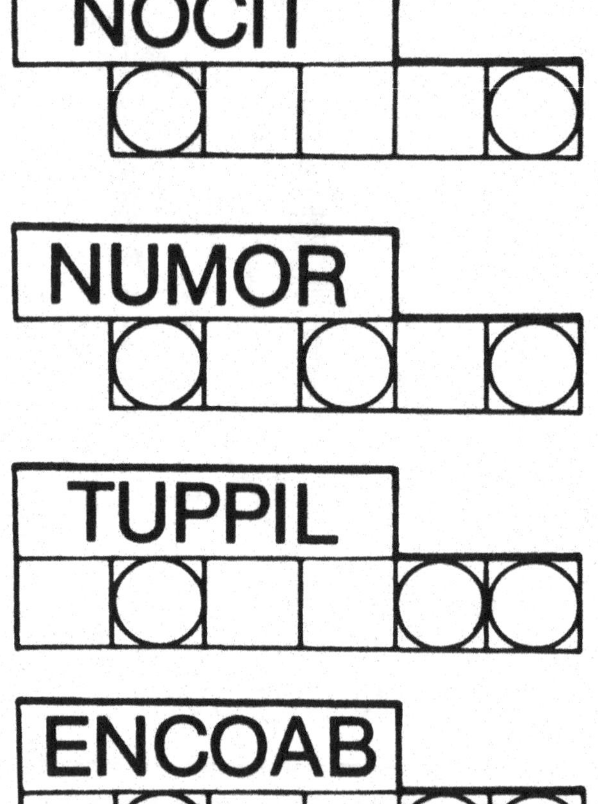

NOCIT
NUMOR
TUPPIL
ENCOAB

Doesn't waste time
HE BECAME MAN OF THE HOUR BECAUSE HE KNEW HOW TO MAKE THIS.

Now arrange the circled letters to form the surprise answer, as suggested by the above cartoon.

Answer: EVERY

101

JUMBLE®

Unscramble these four Jumbles, one letter to each square, to form four ordinary words.

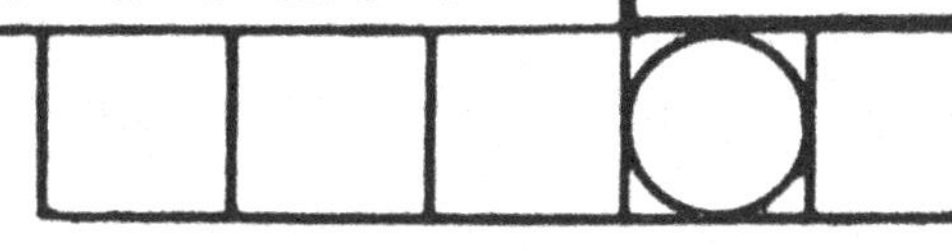
YORIN

GERAW

DEBOHL

RAFAIN

WHAT ACCORDION MUSIC MIGHT SOMETIMES BE.

Now arrange the circled letters to form the surprise answer, as suggested by the above cartoon.

Answer here: 
OUT

102

JUMBLE®

Unscramble these four Jumbles, one letter to each square, to form four ordinary words.

FAHFC

DUESE

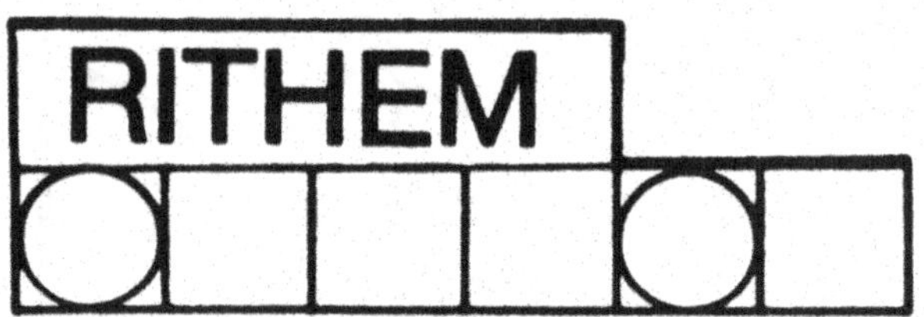
RITHEM

GLUNOE

She hit the ceiling with that one
WHAT THE SOPRANO'S "SOLO" WAS.

Now arrange the circled letters to form the surprise answer, as suggested by the above cartoon.

Print answer here: 

103

JUMBLE®

Unscramble these four Jumbles, one letter to each square, to form four ordinary words.

POCUE

FROOG

TENNIT

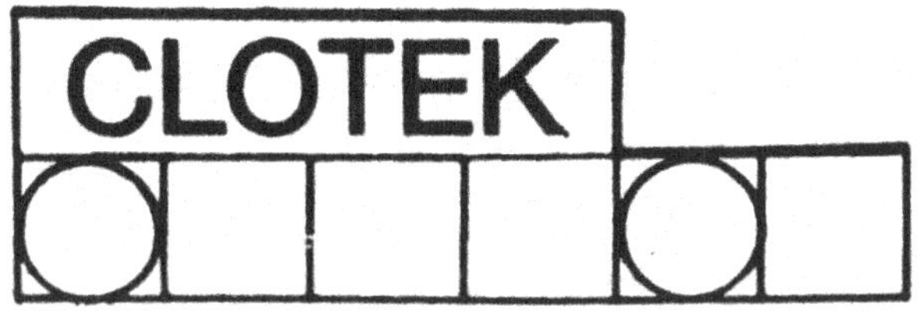
CLOTEK

ALWAYS THE CENTER OF ATTENTION.

Now arrange the circled letters to form the surprise answer, as suggested by the above cartoon.

Print answer here: THE 

104

JUMBLE®

Unscramble these four Jumbles, one letter to each square, to form four ordinary words.

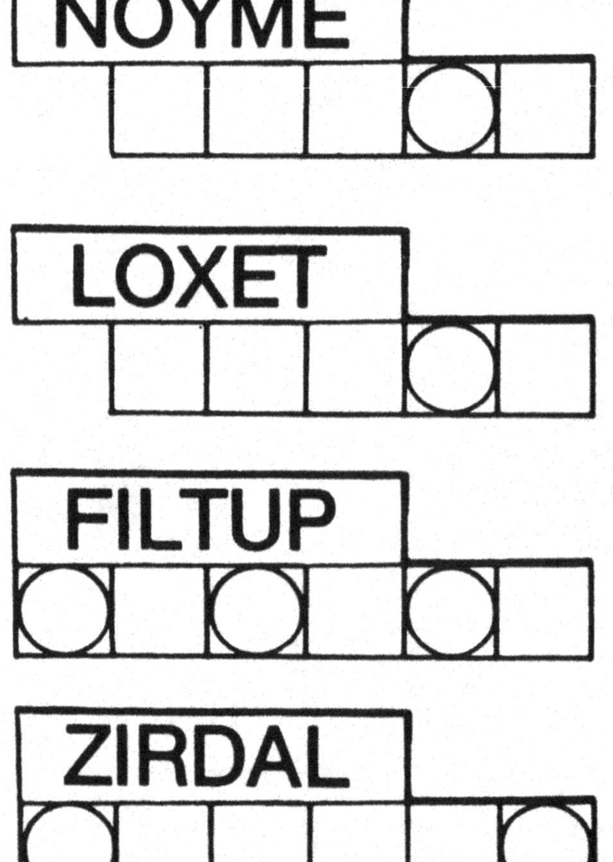
NOYME
LOXET
FILTUP
ZIRDAL

THEY CALLED THE COMEDIAN A "GAS," BECAUSE HE WAS THIS.

Now arrange the circled letters to form the surprise answer, as suggested by the above cartoon.

Answer here: JUST AN ◯◯◯ "◯◯◯◯"

105

JUMBLE®

Unscramble these four Jumbles, one letter to each square, to form four ordinary words.

TRINP
MAITY
LEMAFE

DORIAH

I have a lovely table for you
TALKS WITHOUT GIVING ITSELF AWAY.

Now arrange the circled letters to form the surprise answer, as suggested by the above cartoon.

Print answer here: 

106

JUMBLE®

Unscramble these four Jumbles, one letter to each square, to form four ordinary words.

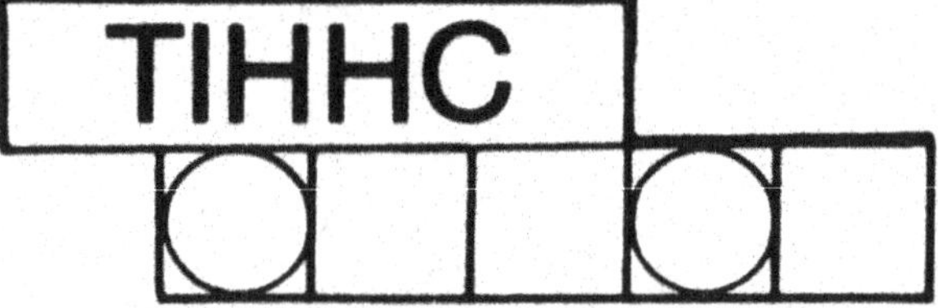
TIHHC

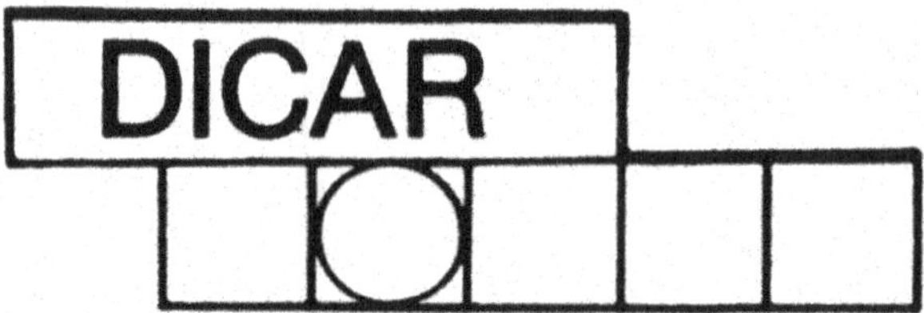
DICAR

MIENER

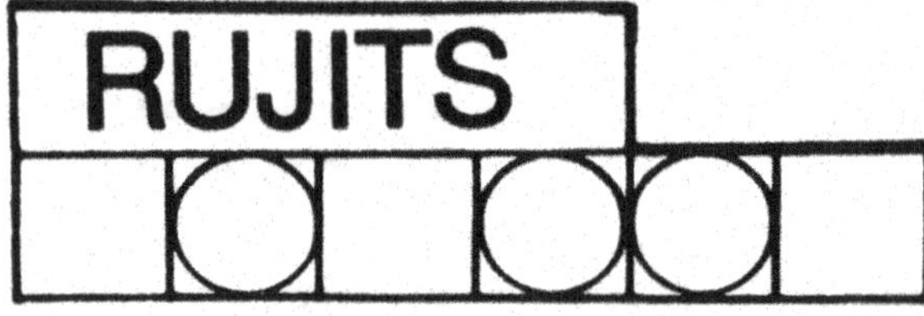
RUJITS

WHAT THE
VIOLINIST
WAS UP TO.

Now arrange the circled letters to form the surprise answer, as suggested by the above cartoon.

Answer: HIS ◯◯◯◯ IN ◯◯◯◯◯

107

JUMBLE®

Unscramble these four Jumbles, one letter to each square, to form four ordinary words.

EVVAL

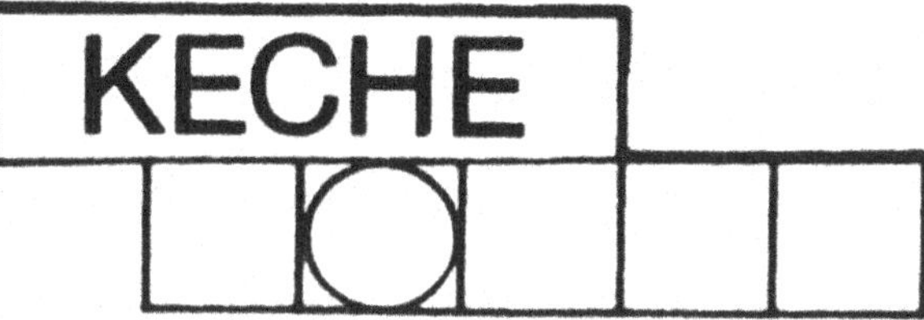
KECHE

IBBART

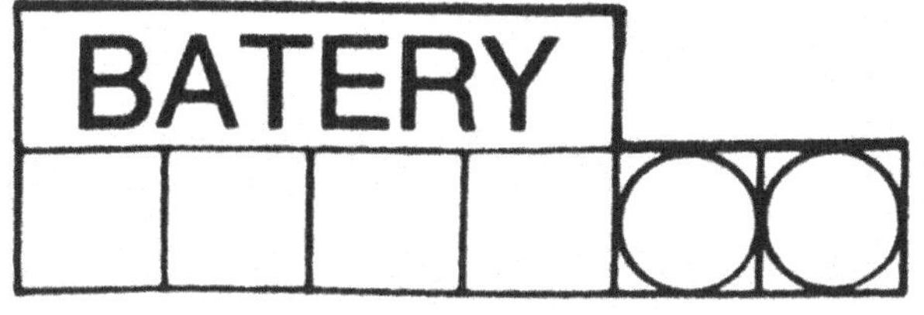
BATERY

HOW THEY GREETED EACH OTHER AT THE CARDIOLOGISTS' ANNUAL SHINDIG.

Now arrange the circled letters to form the surprise answer, as suggested by the above cartoon.

Print answer here: 

108

JUMBLE®

Unscramble these four Jumbles, one letter to each square, to form four ordinary words.

OMIDI

AWNTY

COBIXE

YERRSH

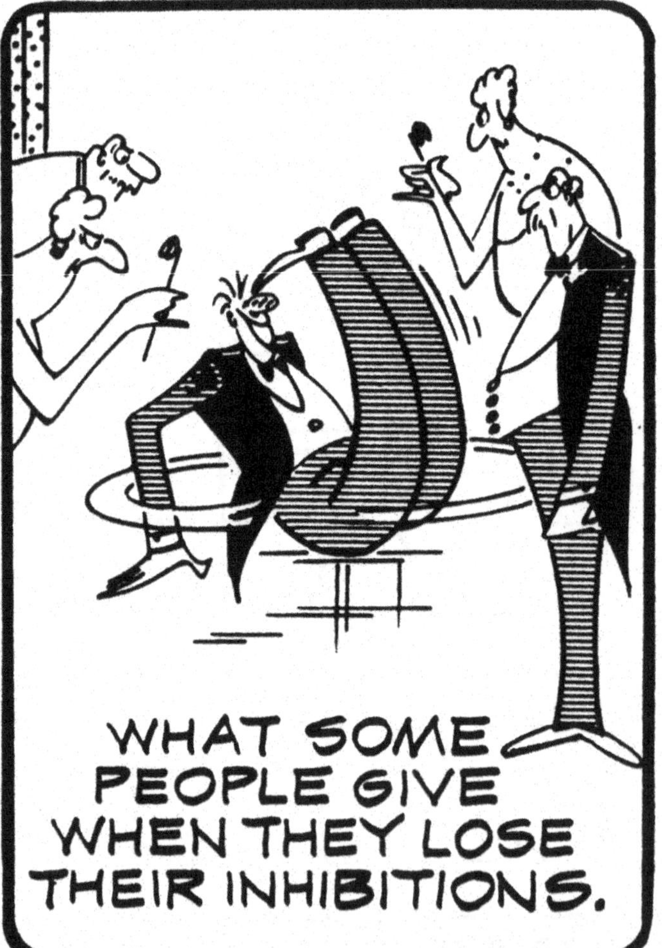
WHAT SOME
PEOPLE GIVE
WHEN THEY LOSE
THEIR INHIBITIONS.

Now arrange the circled letters to form the surprise answer, as suggested by the above cartoon.

Answer:

109

JUMBLE®

Unscramble these four Jumbles, one letter to each square, to form four ordinary words.

YURMK

BROAN

THROXE

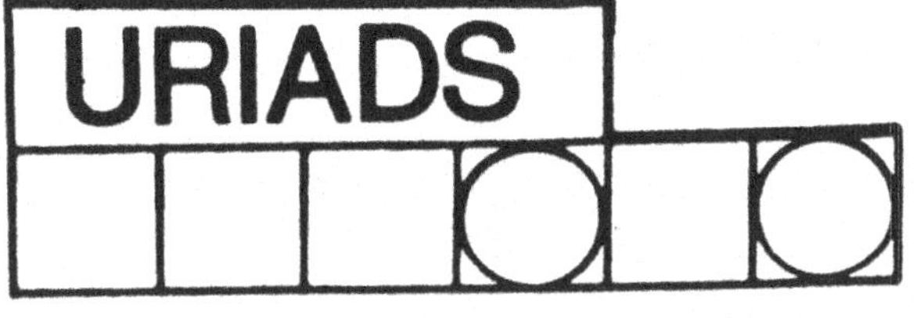
URIADS

WHAT A BRIDGE PLAYER HAS TO LEARN HOW TO DO.

Now arrange the circled letters to form the surprise answer, as suggested by the above cartoon.

Answer here:

IT ON THE

110

JUMBLE®

Unscramble these four Jumbles, one letter to each square, to form four ordinary words.

NEATE

OSOGE

NIMERV

YIELDE

Wish he'd shut up
WHAT SOME PEOPLE DO WHEN THEY HOLD A CONVERSATION.

Now arrange the circled letters to form the surprise answer, as suggested by the above cartoon.

Answer here:

111

JUMBLE®

Unscramble these four Jumbles, one letter to each square, to form four ordinary words.

LEWJE

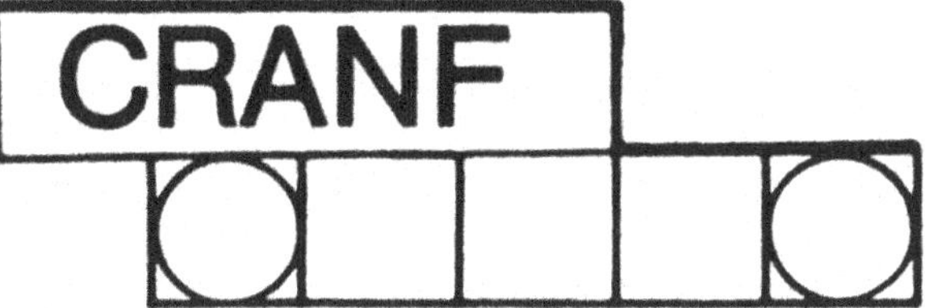
CRANF

THROBE

DEFUAL

YAK
YAK
IF YOU'RE NOT CAREFUL ABOUT LENDING AN EAR YOU MIGHT GET THIS.

Now arrange the circled letters to form the surprise answer, as suggested by the above cartoon.

Answer here: IT 

JUMBLE®

Unscramble these four Jumbles, one letter to each square, to form four ordinary words.

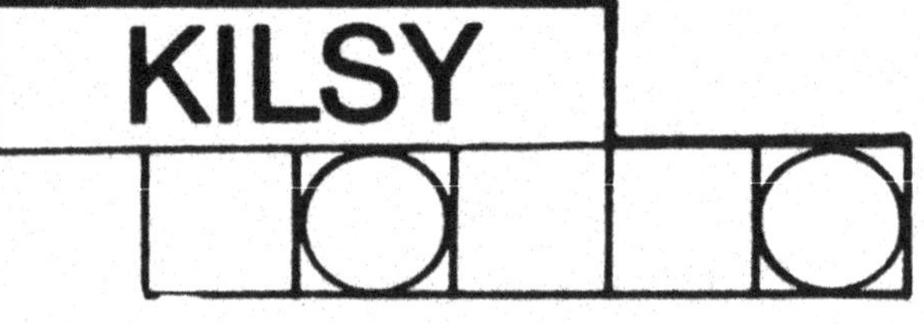
KILSY

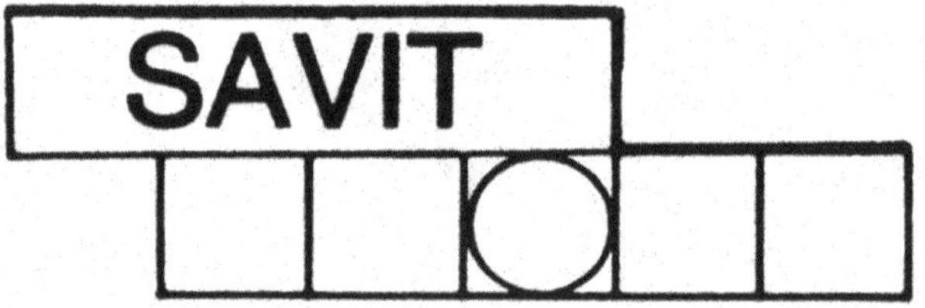
SAVIT

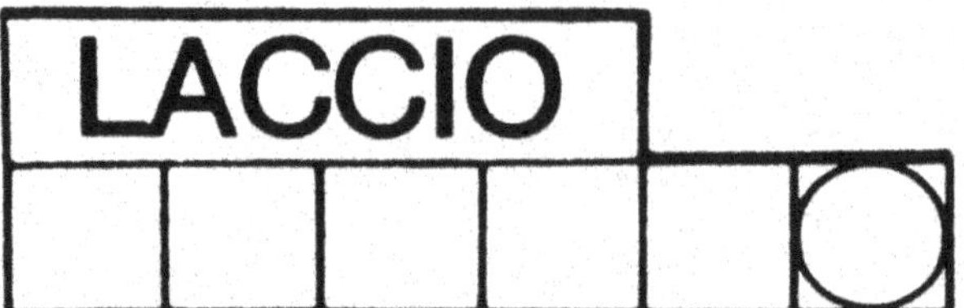
LACCIO

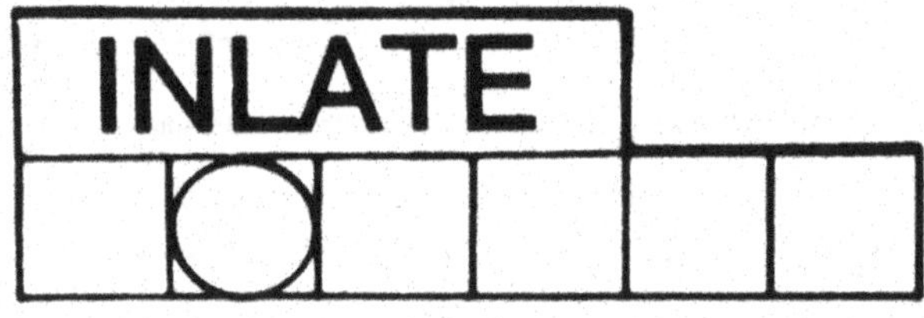
INLATE

A "STILL" IS AN APPARATUS THAT MAKES MANY PEOPLE THIS.

Now arrange the circled letters to form the surprise answer, as suggested by the above cartoon.

Print answer here: "  "

113

JUMBLE®

Unscramble these four Jumbles, one letter to each square, to form four ordinary words.

HOOPT

DAFEM

DECAFE

LAWHOL

Now, now—listen to reason
THE BEST THING TO HAVE IN A HEATED DISCUSSION.

Now arrange the circled letters to form the surprise answer, as suggested by the above cartoon.

Print answer here: A 

114

JUMBLE®

Unscramble these four Jumbles, one letter to each square, to form four ordinary words.

BOYTO

YAFOR

TREMIC

DEMPIN

Ugh!
WHAT SOME MUSICAL PERFOR-MANCES SOUND LIKE SOMEONE'S HAVING.

Now arrange the circled letters to form the surprise answer, as suggested by the above cartoon.

Answer: AN "◯◯◯◯◯-◯◯◯◯"

115

JUMBLE®

Unscramble these four Jumbles, one letter to each square, to form four ordinary words.

INLOG

YORRS

CUDINT

NERKUB

Ugh!
HE WAS SO HEALTHY IT WAS THIS.

Now arrange the circled letters to form the surprise answer, as suggested by the above cartoon.

Answer here: "  "

116

JUMBLE®

Unscramble these four Jumbles, one letter to each square, to form four ordinary words.

TELIT

RADAW

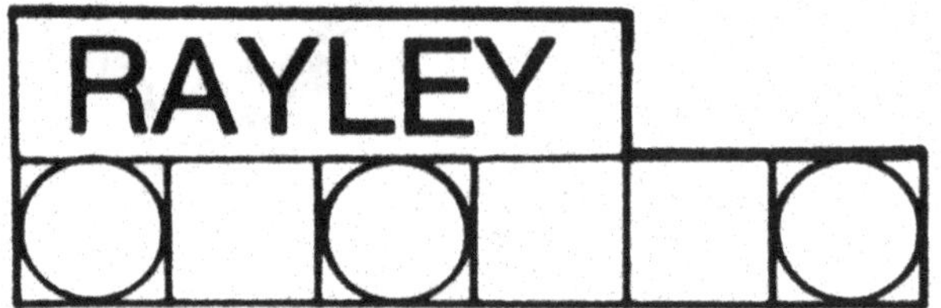
RAYLEY

VIRFED

MILK
A CONFIRMED NIGHT OWL IS A MAN WHO STAYS UP ALL NIGHT—

Now arrange the circled letters to form the surprise answer, as suggested by the above cartoon.

Answer: ◯◯◯ ◯◯◯◯◯ ◯◯◯

117

JUMBLE®

Unscramble these four Jumbles, one letter to each square, to form four ordinary words.

NOWDY

VOACH

ANCIDD

BLOGIE

Disgraceful!
But interesting!
WHAT SCANDAL HAS TO BE.

Now arrange the circled letters to form the surprise answer, as suggested by the above cartoon.

Print answer here:  TO BE 

118

JUMBLE®

Unscramble these four Jumbles, one letter to each square, to form four ordinary words.

YEDIT

DAULT

FISHTE

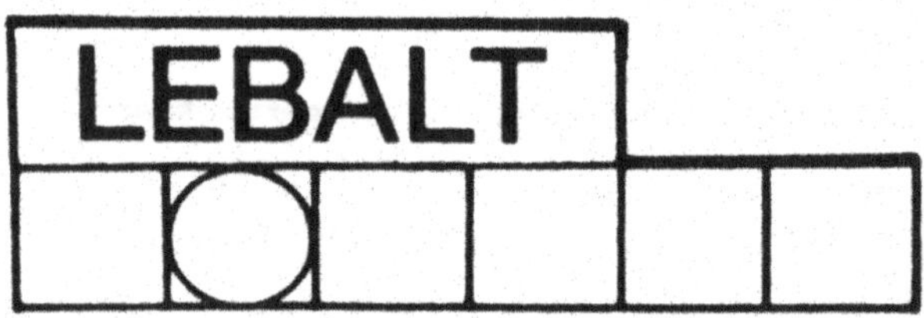
LEBALT

And to make a long story short. . .
Wish he'd come to the point
WHAT "TALES" TOLD BY A LONG-WINDED BORE USUALLY HAVE TOO MANY OF.

Now arrange the circled letters to form the surprise answer, as suggested by the above cartoon.

Print answer here:

119

JUMBLE®

Unscramble these four Jumbles, one letter to each square, to form four ordinary words.

FREVE

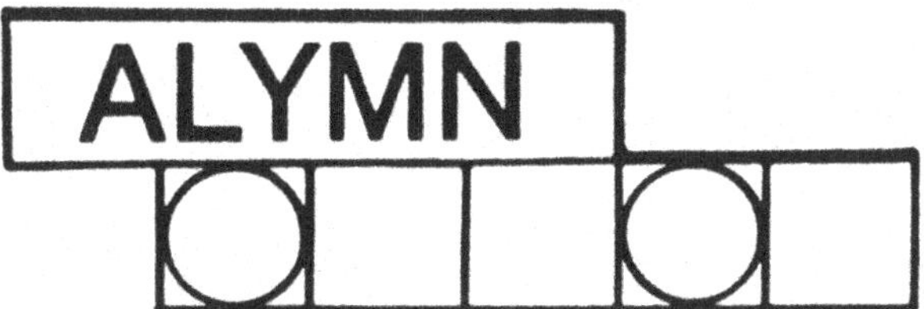
ALYMN

YARBEK

THELAH

WHAT THEY CALLED THAT CLASSY NEW ART GALLERY.

Now arrange the circled letters to form the surprise answer, as suggested by the above cartoon.

Answer: THE ◯◯◯◯ OF ◯◯◯◯◯

120

JUMBLE®

Unscramble these four Jumbles, one letter to each square, to form four ordinary words.

TOIDT

LAASI

CHALUN

UPLARB

WHAT KIND OF JOKES DO THOSE MOUNTAIN FOLK TELL?

Now arrange the circled letters to form the surprise answer, as suggested by the above cartoon.

Answer: "[ ][ ][ ][ ]-[ ][ ][ ][ ][ ][ ]" ONES

121

JUMBLE®

Unscramble these four Jumbles, one letter to each square, to form four ordinary words.

LAUDT

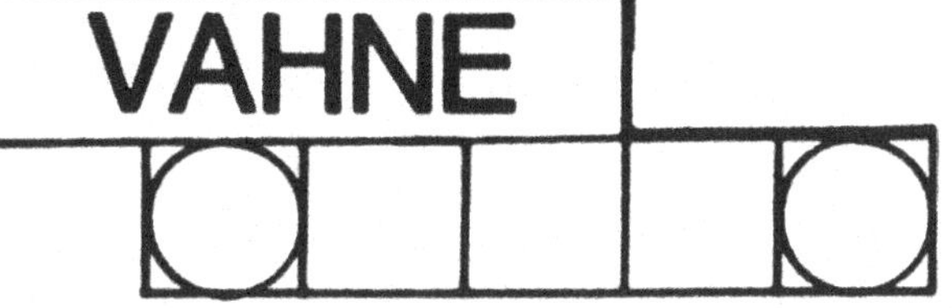
VAHNE

YARNLE

FACEEF

You're getting it
DANCE
WHAT A GOOD DANCER HAS TO BE.

Now arrange the circled letters to form the surprise answer, as suggested by the above cartoon.

Answer: “ ” WITH HIS

122

JUMBLE®

Unscramble these four Jumbles, one letter to each square, to form four ordinary words.

MUTON

TOQUA

UNBRAU

AGCUTH

Somebody better put a stop to this or he's going to be sorry
THAT OFFENSIVE TALKER HAD A TONGUE SO SHARP HE ALMOST DID THIS.

Now arrange the circled letters to form the surprise answer, as suggested by the above cartoon.

Answer here:  HIS OWN 

123

JUMBLE®

Unscramble these four Jumbles, one letter to each square, to form four ordinary words.

GLIBE

TABOU

LARREY

DIFLED

WHAT A MAN
GIVEN TO HORSE-
LAUGHS SHOULD BE.

Now arrange the circled letters to form the surprise answer, as suggested by the above cartoon.

Print answer here: 

124

JUMBLE®

Unscramble these four Jumbles, one letter to each square, to form four ordinary words.

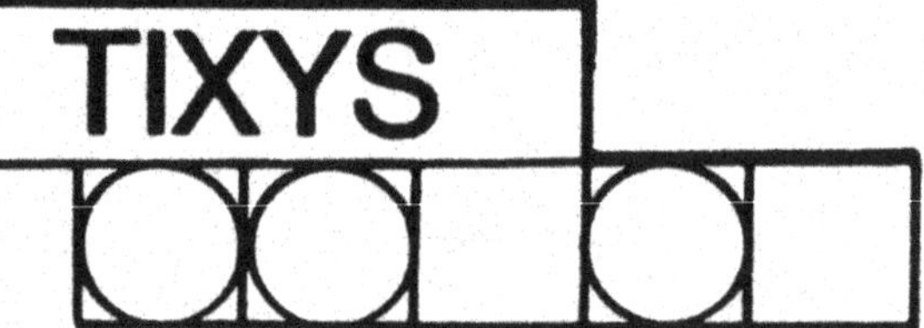
TIXYS

ROAPE

STYJUL

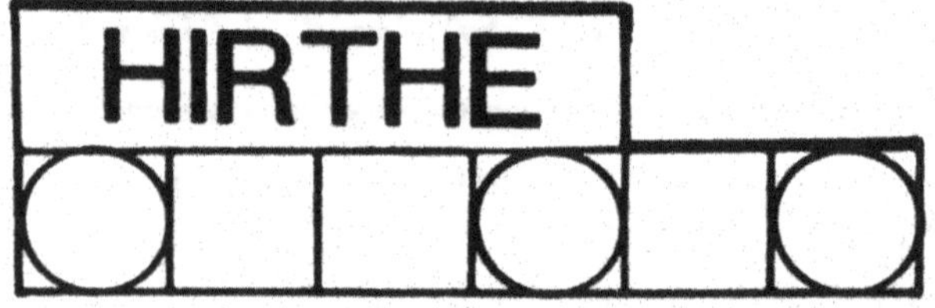
HIRTHE

WHEN YOU OPEN YOUR MOUTH TO YAWN, IT COULD BE A HINT TO OTHERS TO DO THIS.

Now arrange the circled letters to form the surprise answer, as suggested by the above cartoon.

Answer here:

125

JUMBLE®

Unscramble these four Jumbles, one letter to each square, to form four ordinary words.

VELOR

ENWIC

SHUPTY

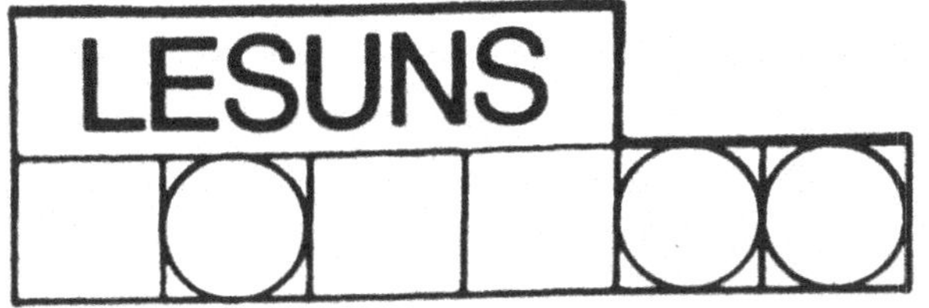
LESUNS

A SCANDALMONGER IS MOST HAPPY WHEN SHE CONFESSES THIS.

Now arrange the circled letters to form the surprise answer, as suggested by the above cartoon.

Answer: THE ◯◯◯◯ OF ◯◯◯◯◯◯

126

JUMBLE®

Unscramble these four Jumbles, one letter to each square, to form four ordinary words.

MOECT

FINEK

RUJINO

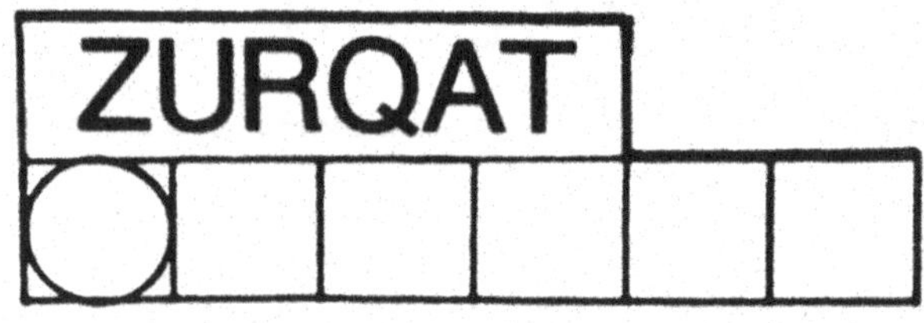
ZURQAT

YAK YAK YAK
A GUY SHOULD BE THIS WHEN HE GOES ON A DIET.

Now arrange the circled letters to form the surprise answer, as suggested by the above cartoon.

Print answer here:

127

JUMBLE®

Unscramble these four Jumbles, one letter to each square, to form four ordinary words.

FLONE

SYRTT

CRADOW

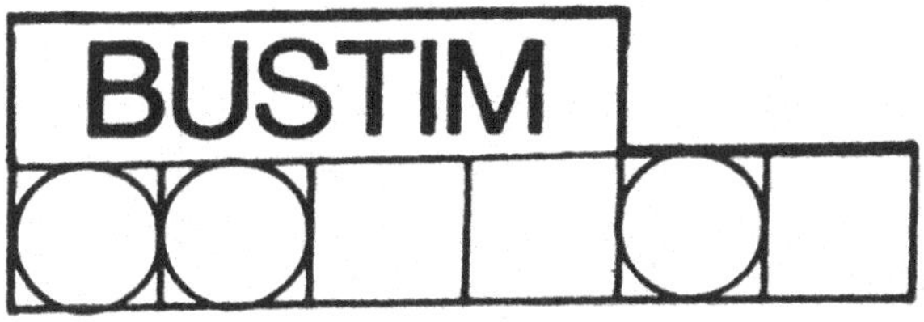
BUSTIM

AT MOST BANQUETS THIS IS THE MAIN COURSE.

Now arrange the circled letters to form the surprise answer, as suggested by the above cartoon.

Print answer here: 

JUMBLE®

Unscramble these four Jumbles, one letter to each square, to form four ordinary words.

RYTUL

KADEB

SEJERY

PLINEP

This'll wow 'em!

WHAT THE AUDIENCE GAVE HIM WHEN HE WAS EXPECTING CHEERS.

Now arrange the circled letters to form the surprise answer, as suggested by the above cartoon.

Print answer here:

129

JUMBLE®

Unscramble these four Jumbles, one letter to each square, to form four ordinary words.

ONSOW

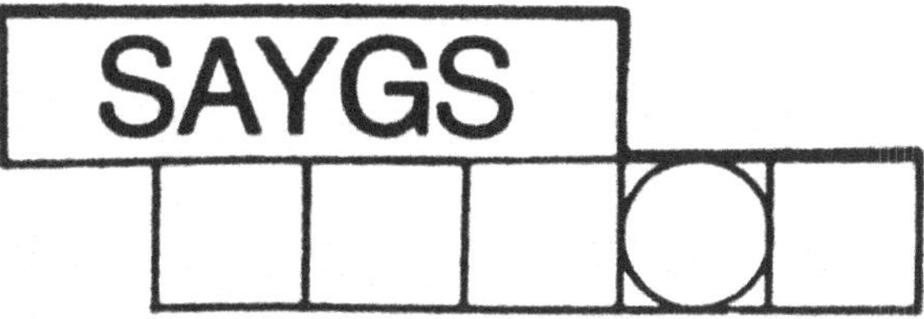
SAYGS

AGNEET

FAINAR

THE MAIN COURSE AT THE COMEDIANS' ANNUAL BANQUET.

Now arrange the circled letters to form the surprise answer, as suggested by the above cartoon.

Print answer here: THE ""

130

JUMBLE®

Unscramble these four Jumbles, one letter to each square, to form four ordinary words.

NIFYN

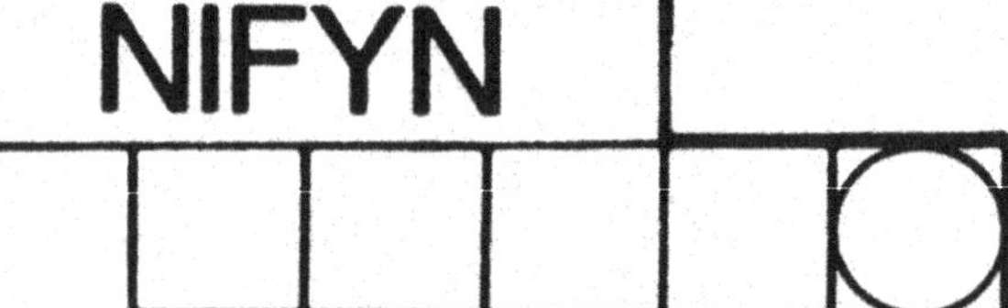

CAPNI

PELSOG

BANACA

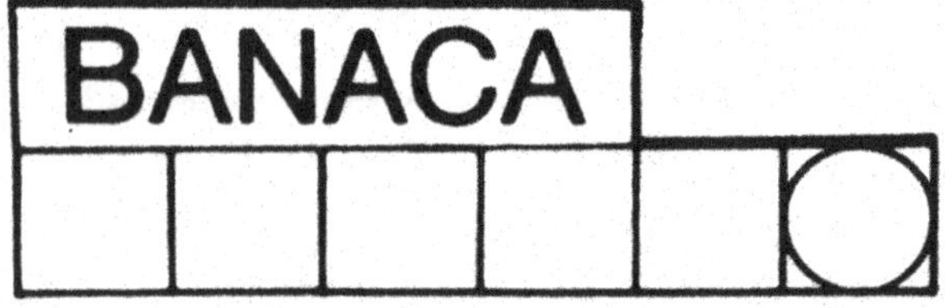

They say he makes a good living off sponging

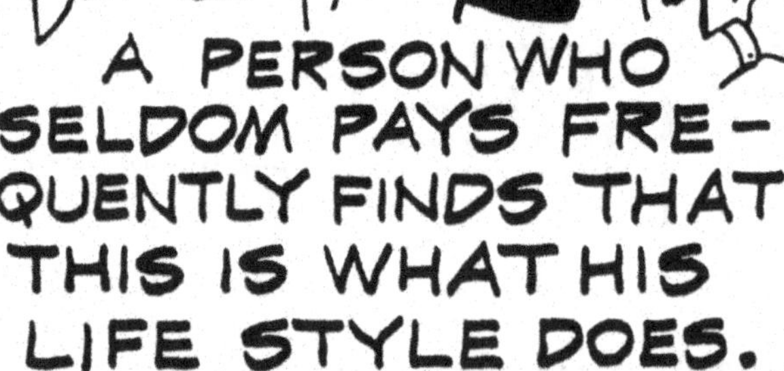
A PERSON WHO SELDOM PAYS FRE-
QUENTLY FINDS THAT
THIS IS WHAT HIS
LIFE STYLE DOES.

Now arrange the circled letters to form the surprise answer, as suggested by the above cartoon.

Print answer here: "  "

131

JUMBLE®

Unscramble these four Jumbles, one letter to each square, to form four ordinary words.

PONCA

TRYNE

UNSLIM

GEDDUR

And now for the storybook ending
HE DOESN'T UNDERSTAND THAT HIS WIFE DOES---

Now arrange the circled letters to form the surprise answer, as suggested by the above cartoon.

Answer here: 
HIM

132

JUMBLE®

Unscramble these four Jumbles, one letter to each square, to form four ordinary words.

KOYLE

ENZOO

YOPMIC

TURTEG

"SOCIETY" WAS WHERE YOUNG WOMEN STARTED IN BY---

Now arrange the circled letters to form the surprise answer, as suggested by the above cartoon.

Answer here: " ______ ___ "

133

JUMBLE®

Unscramble these four Jumbles, one letter to each square, to form four ordinary words.

SOYUM

USSOE

GRUFIE

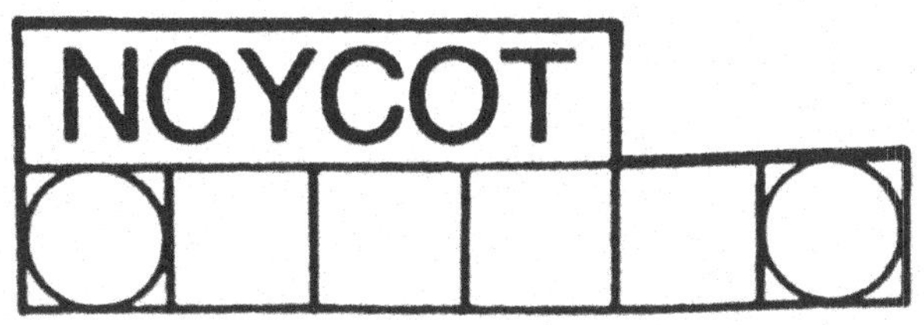
NOYCOT

ONE OF THE VERY FEW PLACES WHERE A WOMAN MIGHT WEAR A HAT THESE DAYS.

Now arrange the circled letters to form the surprise answer, as suggested by the above cartoon.

Print answer here: IN  OF 

134

JUMBLE®

Unscramble these four Jumbles, one letter to each square, to form four ordinary words.

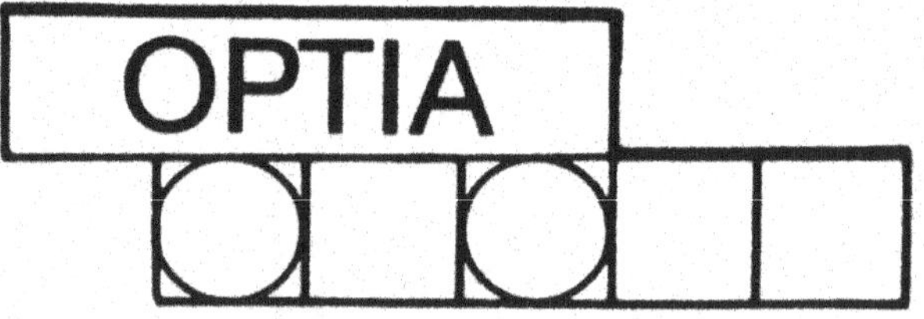
OPTIA

HACCO

KRUTEY

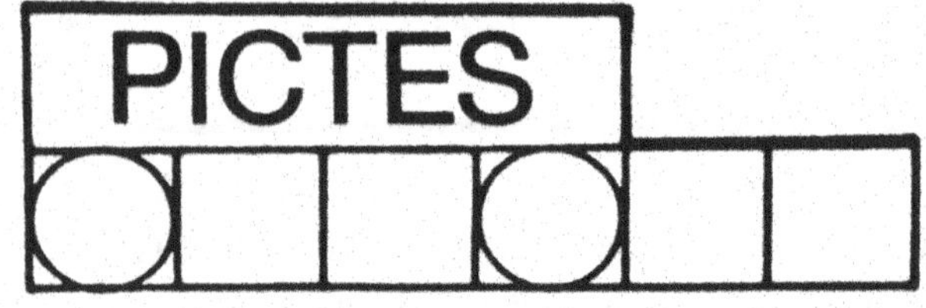
PICTES

Shh!

SAVING ONE'S FACE IS OFTEN A MATTER OF KEEPING ---

Now arrange the circled letters to form the surprise answer, as suggested by the above cartoon.

Print answer here:

OF
IT

135

JUMBLE®

Unscramble these four Jumbles, one letter to each square, to form four ordinary words.

MILPE

LYDIO

REYJES

DINNAL

Look who's handing out advice

A PERSON WHO IS CONSTANTLY GIVING OTHERS A PIECE OF HIS MIND USUALLY HAS THIS.

Now arrange the circled letters to form the surprise answer, as suggested by the above cartoon.

Answer here:

TO

136

JUMBLE®

Unscramble these four Jumbles, one letter to each square, to form four ordinary words.

LUFET

EXVIN

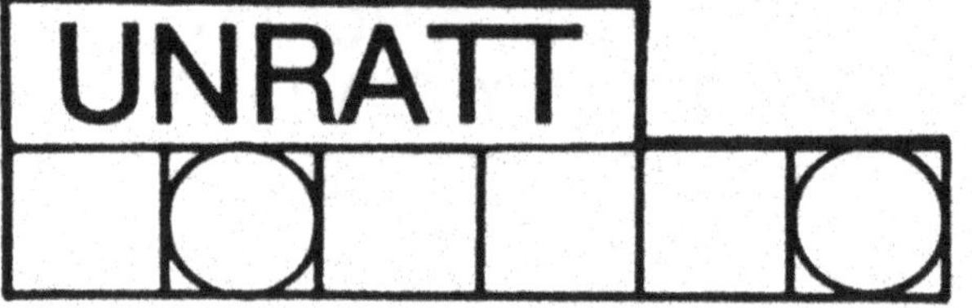
UNRATT

CHAPER

As I was saying
YAK YAK YAK YAK
Time to go, dear
THE BEST WAY TO MAKE A LONG STORY SHORT.

Now arrange the circled letters to form the surprise answer, as suggested by the above cartoon.

Answer here:  HIM

137

JUMBLE.

Unscramble these four Jumbles, one letter to each square, to form four ordinary words.

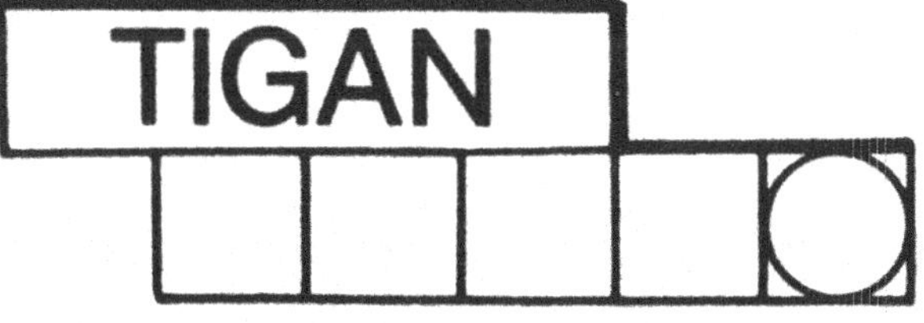
TIGAN

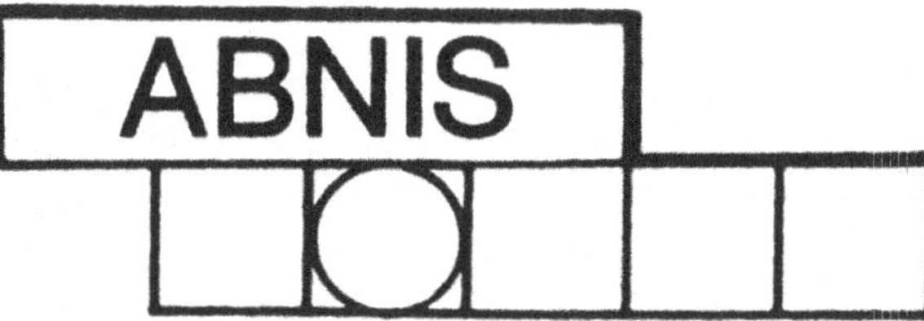
ABNIS

STUBOE

WOLTAL

OFTEN DRUNK BUT NEVER INTOXICATED.

Now arrange the circled letters to form the surprise answer, as suggested by the above cartoon.

Print answer here:

138

JUMBLE.®

Unscramble these four Jumbles, one letter to each square, to form four ordinary words.

NOWNK

WULAF

FOLFAY

PEKAUM

I'm m-m-making no deshisions at thish time

Time to go home

HE FOUND IT EASIER TO SIT TIGHT THAN THIS.

Now arrange the circled letters to form the surprise answer, as suggested by the above cartoon.

Print answer here:  THAT 

JUMBLE.®

Unscramble these four Jumbles, one letter to each square, to form four ordinary words.

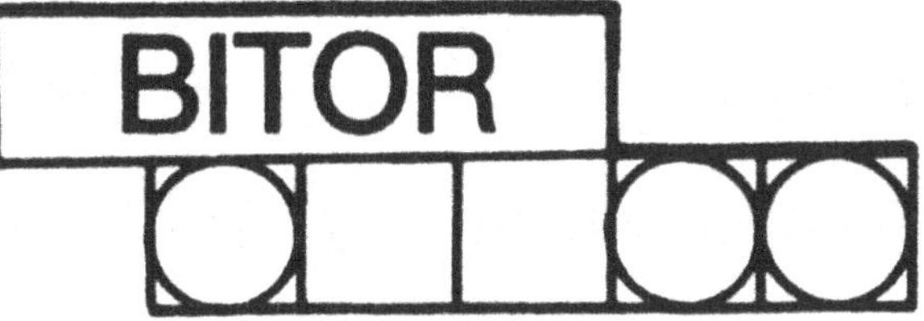
BITOR

MOBOL

UNGOTE

WAYELE

THEIR OLD MAN MADE MONEY IN QUESTIONABLE WAYS, AND NOW THEY'RE ENJOYING THIS.

Now arrange the circled letters to form the surprise answer, as suggested by the above cartoon.

Answer: "□□□□-□□□□□□" GAINS

140

JUMBLE®

Unscramble these four Jumbles, one letter to each square, to form four ordinary words.

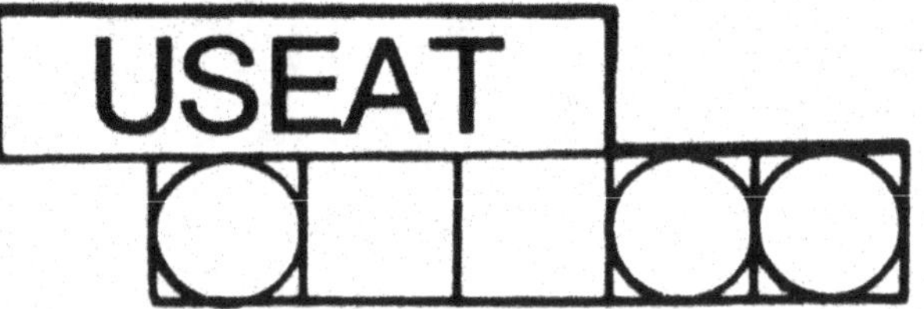
USEAT

RYDYL

PLUCUF

LARULP

WHAT THEY CALL A LOT OF CRUMBS HELD TOGETHER BY THEIR OWN DOUGH.

Now arrange the circled letters to form the surprise answer, as suggested by the above cartoon.

Answer: THE

141

JUMBLE®

Unscramble these four Jumbles, one letter to each square, to form four ordinary words.

CEHOP

FRATE

STANEF

ALCIME

Don't you think you've had enough?

A SELF-INDULGENT GUY NEVER DOES THIS.

Now arrange the circled letters to form the surprise answer, as suggested by the above cartoon.

Answer here: "  " 

142

JUMBLE®

Unscramble these four Jumbles, one letter to each square, to form four ordinary words.

TREXE

NIRAY

MINDOO

SECCAR

Champagne and caviar for everybody!

Here we go again!

MANY A WOMAN THINKS SHE IS FOND OF SPORTS UNTIL SHE DOES THIS.

Now arrange the circled letters to form the surprise answer, as suggested by the above cartoon.

Answer here:

143

JUMBLE®

Unscramble these four Jumbles, one letter to each square, to form four ordinary words.

RONED

GHEED

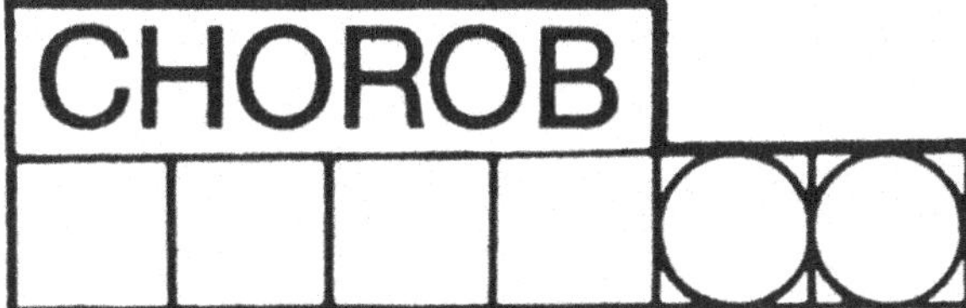
CHOROB

HOLURY

He pockets plenty

WHAT THE BAKER TURNED COMEDIAN KNEW HOW TO MAKE.

Now arrange the circled letters to form the surprise answer, as suggested by the above cartoon.

Answer: ◯◯◯◯◯ OUT OF "◯◯◯◯◯"

144

JUMBLE®

Unscramble these four Jumbles, one letter to each square, to form four ordinary words.

VOPER

AMLET

FISHTE

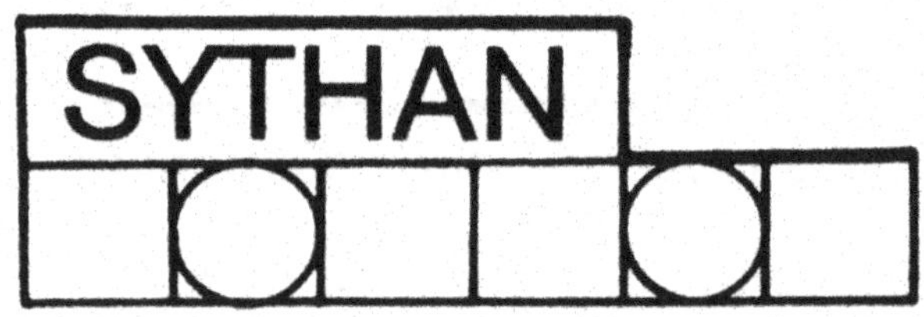
SYTHAN

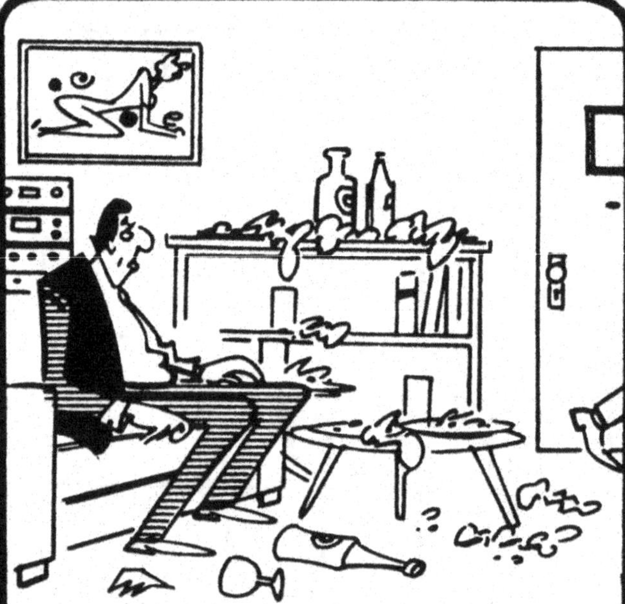
WHAT THEY CALL THAT GUY WHO ALWAYS RE-MAINS AT A PARTY AFTER THE FOOD AND DRINK ARE ALL GONE.

Now arrange the circled letters to form the surprise answer, as suggested by the above cartoon.

Print answer here: 

145

JUMBLE®

Unscramble these four Jumbles, one letter to each square, to form four ordinary words.

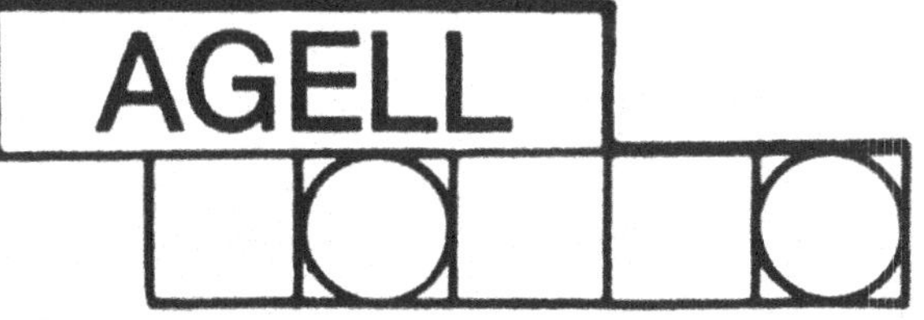
AGELL

HANEY

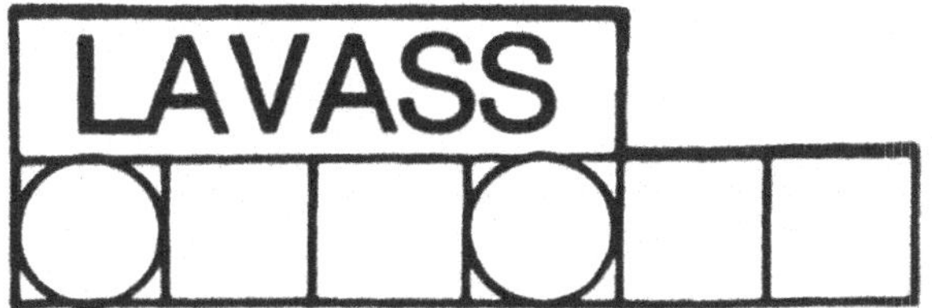
LAVASS

BELEEF

SOME FASHIONS
ARE CUT TO THIS.

Now arrange the circled letters to form the surprise answer, as suggested by the above cartoon.

Print answer here: "  " 

146

JUMBLE®

Unscramble these four Jumbles, one letter to each square, to form four ordinary words.

GLAVE

ILVIC

RANLYX

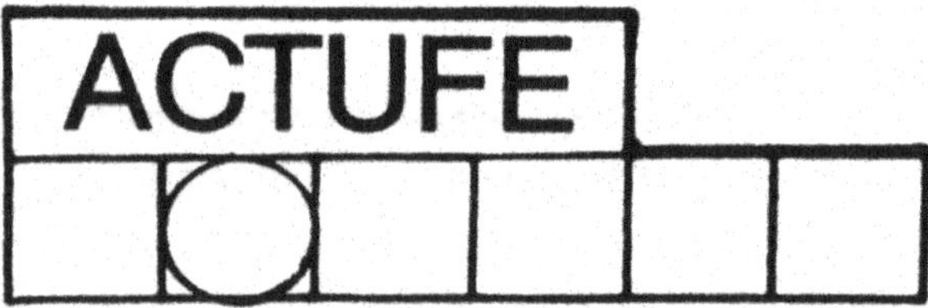
ACTUFE

We'll be pooped tomorrow
Who cares?
SOME PEOPLE WHO GO "ALL OUT" OFTEN END UP---

Now arrange the circled letters to form the surprise answer, as suggested by the above cartoon.

Print answer here: "   "

147

JUMBLE®

Unscramble these four Jumbles, one letter to each square, to form four ordinary words.

UPTYT

ROGIN

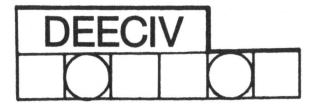

DEECIV

SCOMAT

I want you to meet some friends of mine. They don't have much money, but they're lots of fun

THE OPPORTUNIST HAS NO USE FOR FRIENDS---

Now arrange the circled letters to form the surprise answer, as suggested by the above cartoon.

Print answer here: HE

148

JUMBLE®

Unscramble these four Jumbles, one letter to each square, to form four ordinary words.

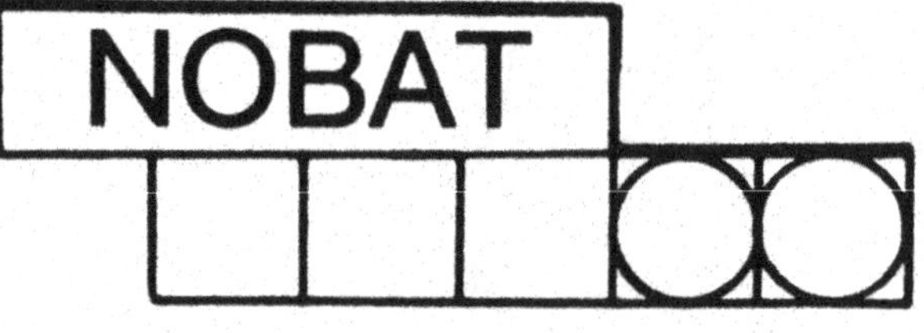
NOBAT

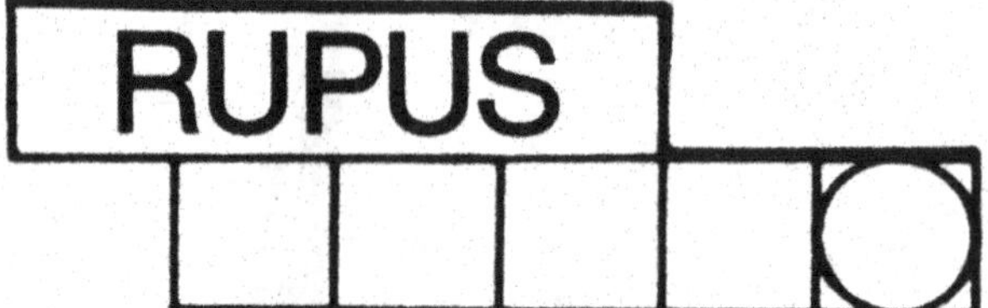
RUPUS

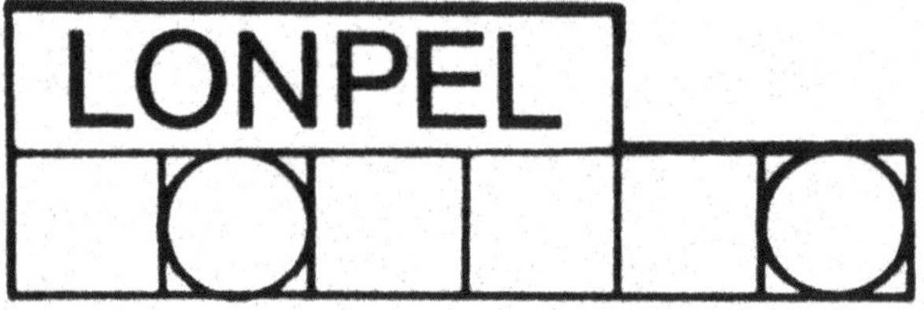
LONPEL

UNGOAT

Ignorance is bliss
THAT OPINIONATED GUY WAS ALWAYS DOWN ON ANY-THING---

Now arrange the circled letters to form the surprise answer, as suggested by the above cartoon.

Answer here: HE WAS  "  " 

149

JUMBLE®

Unscramble these four Jumbles, one letter to each square, to form four ordinary words.

ROVIY

GEWIH

YILSAM

PIGNUM

THAT PATHOLOGICAL LIAR TELLS THE TRUTH ONLY WHEN HIS---

Now arrange the circled letters to form the surprise answer, as suggested by the above cartoon.

Answer:  AREN'T 

150

JUMBLE®

Unscramble these four Jumbles, one letter to each square, to form four ordinary words.

ZOONE

GRITE

MAULSY

TURIAL

WHAT SOME MUSIC GETS WHEN YOU'RE DINING AT A PATRIOTIC BANQUET.

Now arrange the circled letters to form the surprise answer, as suggested by the above cartoon.

Answer: A ▢▢▢▢ ▢▢▢ OF ▢▢▢

151

JUMBLE®

Unscramble these four Jumbles, one letter to each square, to form four ordinary words.

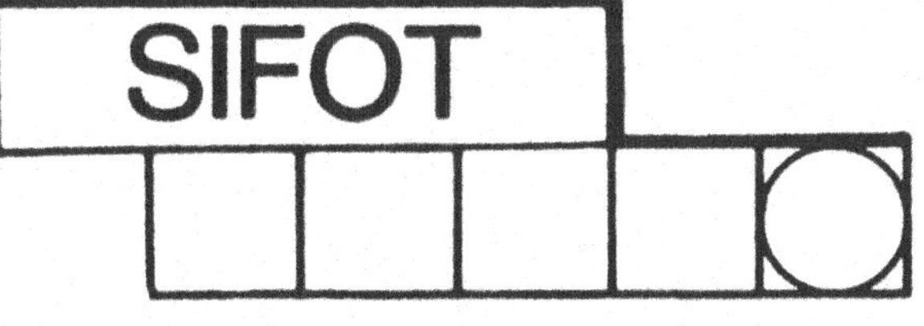
SIFOT

YASES

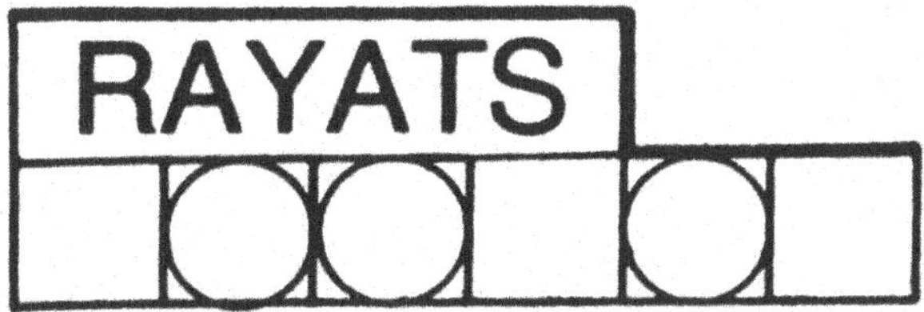
RAYATS

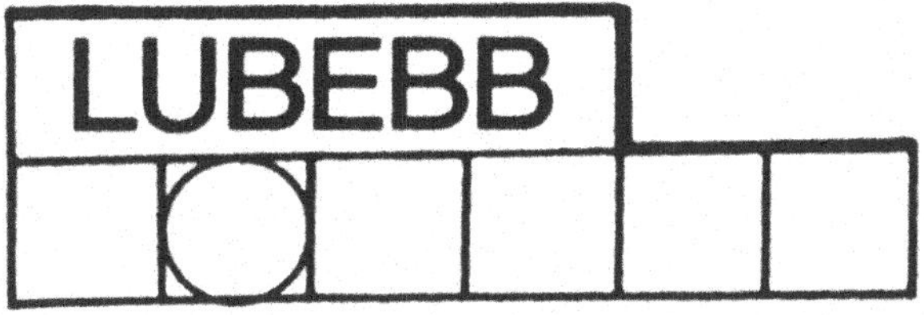
LUBEBB

A social climber, and it looks like he's making it

HE CLIMBED OUT OF HIS "STATUS QUO" IN ORDER TO IMPROVE THIS.

Now arrange the circled letters to form the surprise answer, as suggested by the above cartoon.

Print answer here: HIS 

152

JUMBLE®

Unscramble these four Jumbles, one letter to each square, to form four ordinary words.

REWAY

FEASH

HERNUT

CLISHE

A GOOD POKER
PLAYER CONCEALS
THE KIND OF HAND
HE HAS BY THE
KIND OF FACE---

Now arrange the circled letters to form the surprise answer, as suggested by the above cartoon.

Print answer here:

153

JUMBLE®

Unscramble these four Jumbles, one letter to each square, to form four ordinary words.

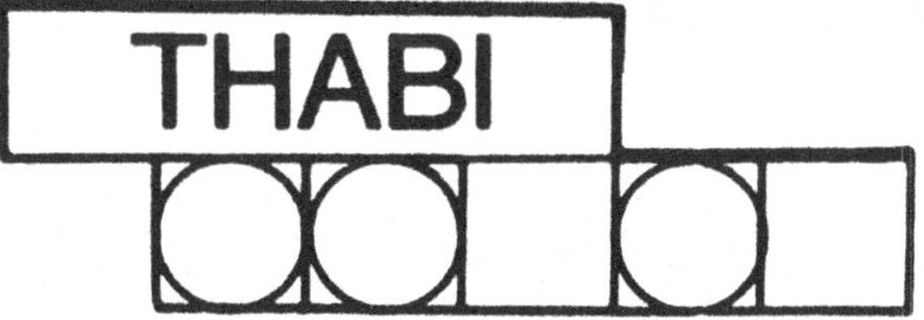
THABI

NEMIR

YIKELL

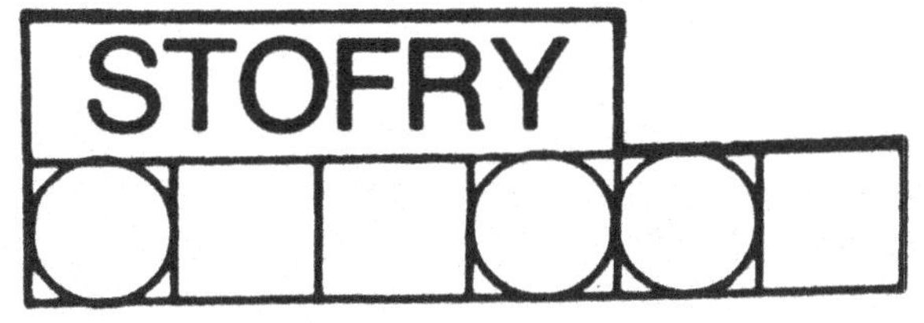
STOFRY

Obnoxious!

HE'S A PERSON ABOUT WHOM YOU'LL NEVER HEAR A GOOD WORD, UNLESS YOU HEAR---

Now arrange the circled letters to form the surprise answer, as suggested by the above cartoon.

Answer: HIM  ABOUT 

154

JUMBLE®

Unscramble these four Jumbles, one letter to each square, to form four ordinary words.

TIHHC

WOGAL

LEMOTE

SNIULF

SUCCESS HASN'T GONE TO HIS HEAD YET---

Now arrange the circled letters to form the surprise answer, as suggested by the above cartoon.

Answer: JUST

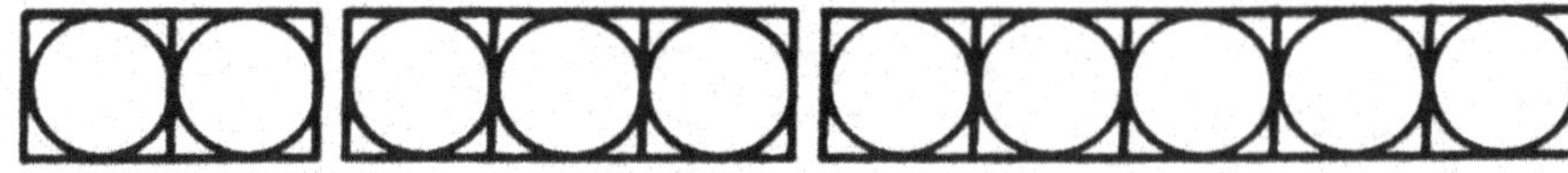

155

JUMBLE®

Unscramble these four Jumbles, one letter to each square, to form four ordinary words.

GUNST

BADIE

LUPCOE

DORWAT

How insulting!
A SHORT "CUTTING" REMARK MAY BE EXPRESSED IN THESE.

Now arrange the circled letters to form the surprise answer, as suggested by the above cartoon.

Answer here: 

156

JUMBLE®

Unscramble these four Jumbles, one letter to each square, to form four ordinary words.

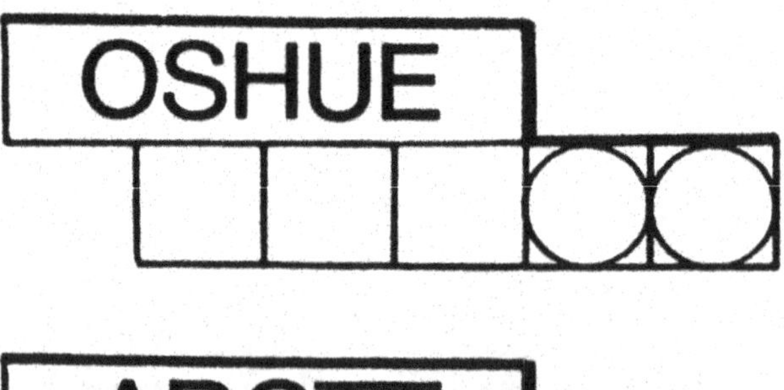
OSHUE

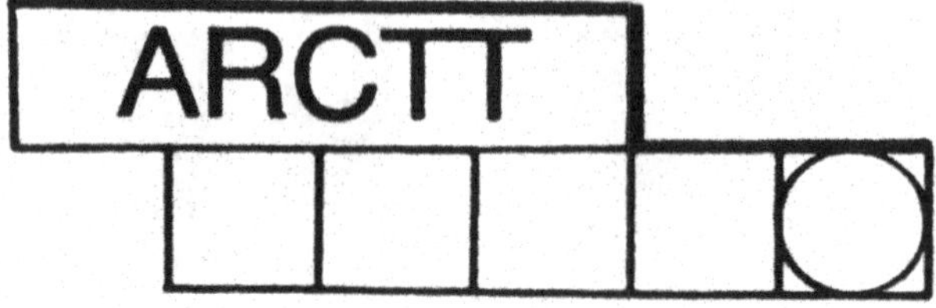
ARCTT

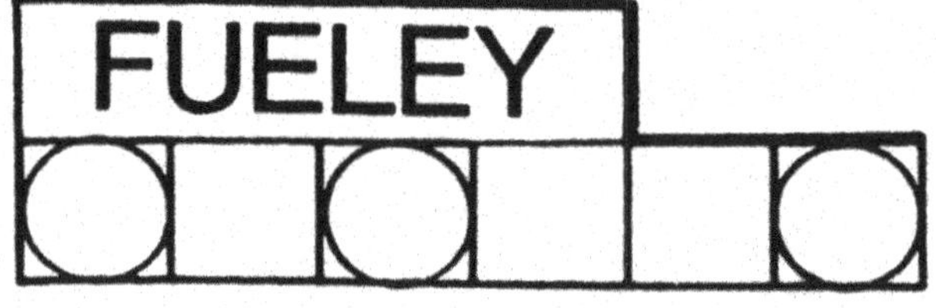
FUELEY

CHISPY

HE ALWAYS ACCOM - PANIED HIS WIFE TO THE OPERA, WHETHER HE NEEDED THIS OR NOT.

Now arrange the circled letters to form the surprise answer, as suggested by the above cartoon.

Print answer here: 

157

JUMBLE®

Unscramble these four Jumbles, one letter to each square, to form four ordinary words.

ENVOW

LEXEP

VACTAR

BYSMOL

She's got my husband!
You've got my hat!
You've got my wife!
SOME PEOPLE WHO ATTEND CONVENTIONS RARELY DO THIS.

Now arrange the circled letters to form the surprise answer, as suggested by the above cartoon.

Answer here:

158

JUMBLE®

Unscramble these four Jumbles, one letter to each square, to form four ordinary words.

RECSS

KLANE

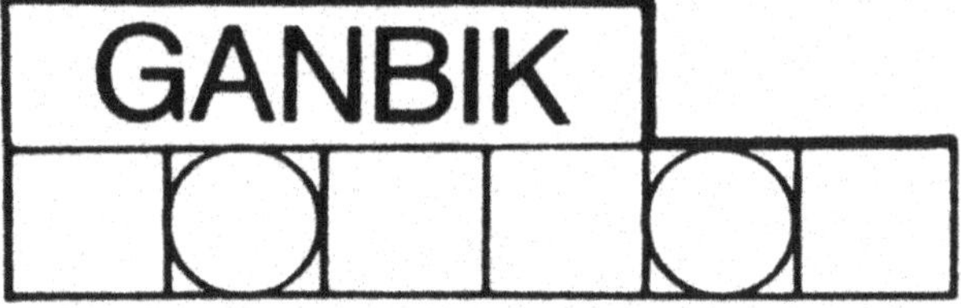
GANBIK

BROMEY

AT WILD PARTIES, "ANYTHING GOES," AND THE FIRST IS USUALLY THIS.

Now arrange the circled letters to form the surprise answer, as suggested by the above cartoon.

Print answer here: 

159

JUMBLE®

Unscramble these four Jumbles, one letter to each square, to form four ordinary words.

SMUNI

ZISEE

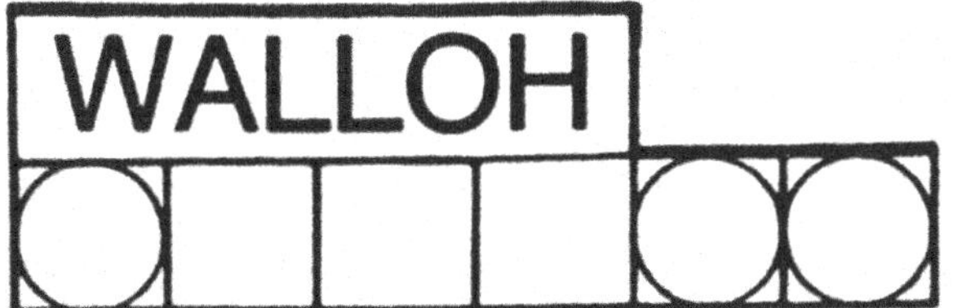
WALLOH

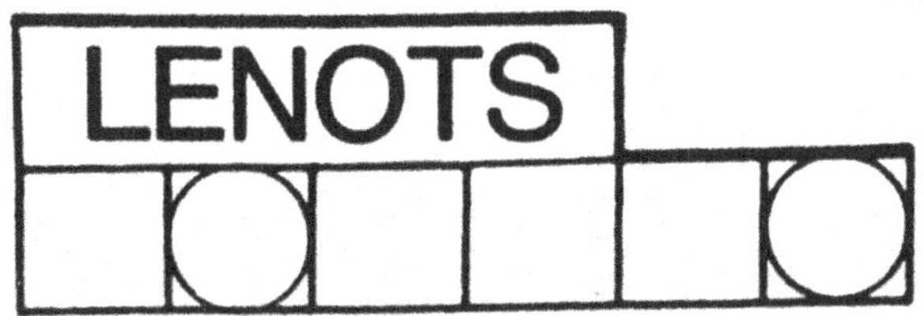
LENOTS

He didn't like her at first
But now it's a different story
A FORTUNE HUNTER DOESN'T REALLY CARE FOR A WOMAN'S COMPANY UNLESS---

Now arrange the circled letters to form the surprise answer, as suggested by the above cartoon.

Answer here: 

JUMBLE®

Unscramble these four Jumbles, one letter to each square, to form four ordinary words.

VOARS

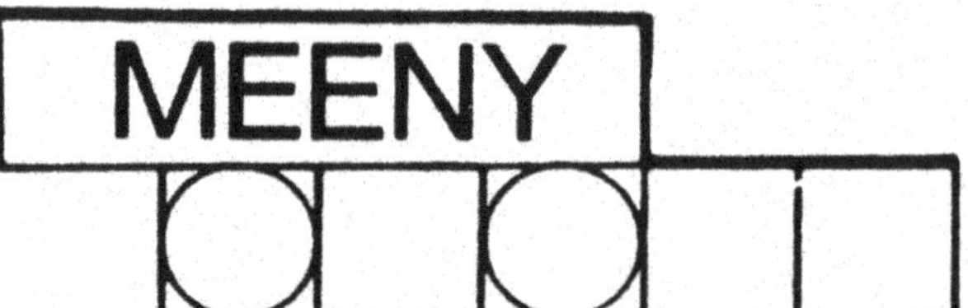
MEENY

FLABEL

YARTIF

Never ever says anything nasty about anyone
A REAL FRIEND KNOCKS BEFORE HE ENTERS---

Now arrange the circled letters to form the surprise answer, as suggested by the above cartoon.

Answer: NOT
HE

161

JUMBLE®

Unscramble these four Jumbles, one letter to each square, to form four ordinary words.

TIVER

KAROC

ZELPUZ

VIRTED

WHAT THEY GAVE THAT GLOOMY LOOKING GUY AT THE PARTY.

Now arrange the circled letters to form the surprise answer, as suggested by the above cartoon.

Answer: THE "◯◯◯◯" ◯◯◯◯◯

162

JUMBLE®

Unscramble these four Jumbles, one letter to each square, to form four ordinary words.

ROATA

PODEK

GLINJE

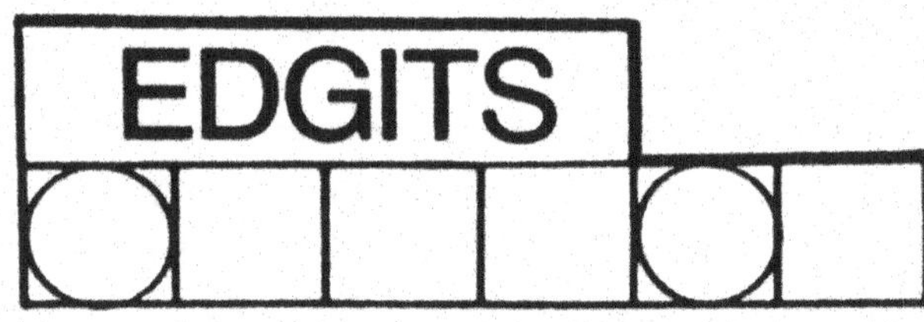
EDGITS

Guess who didn't show up tonight
Yippee !
THAT GROUCH SPREADS GOOD CHEER WHEREVER ---

Now arrange the circled letters to forrn the surprise answer, as suggested by the above cartoon.

Answer here: HE 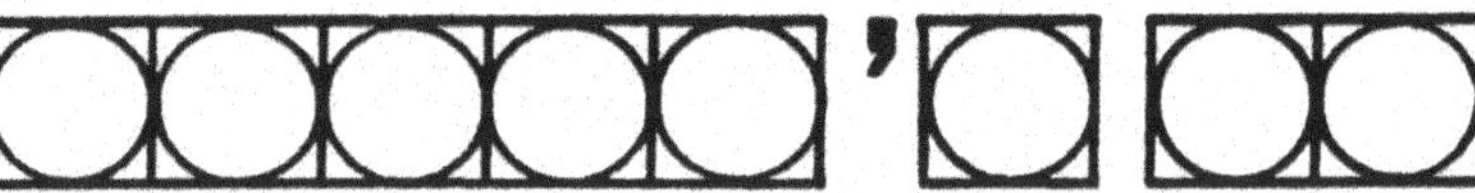

163

JUMBLE®

Unscramble these four Jumbles, one letter to each square, to form four ordinary words.

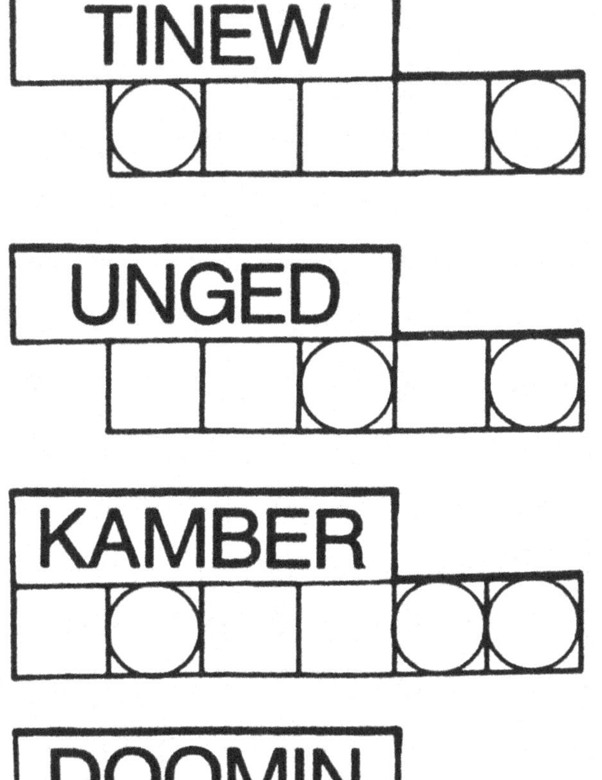
TINEW
UNGED
KAMBER
DOOMIN

WHAT LIFE WAS FOR THE BARFLY.

Now arrange the circled letters to form the surprise answer, as suggested by the above cartoon.

Answer: JUST "▢▢▢▢" & ▢▢▢▢▢▢

164

JUMBLE®

Unscramble these four Jumbles, one letter to each square, to form four ordinary words.

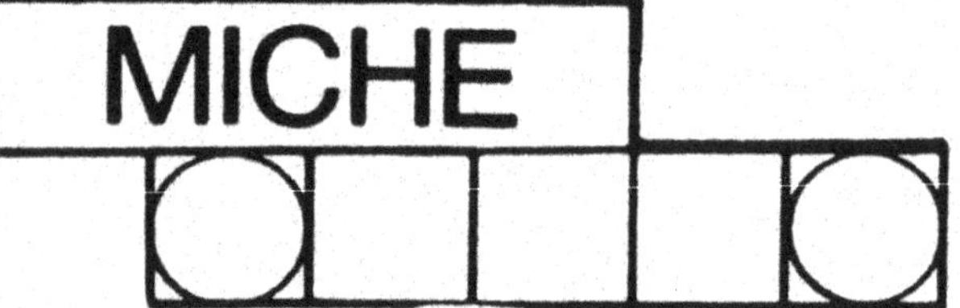
MICHE

TUSEA

CALPEA

HARTHS

Too vain

PEOPLE WHO REFUSE TO WEAR THEIR PRESCRIBED EYE-GLASSES SOMETIMES MAKE THIS OF THEMSELVES.

Now arrange the circled letters to form the surprise answer, as suggested by the above cartoon.

Answer here:

CHALLENGER
JUMBLE
Jubilee

165

JUMBLE®

Unscramble these six Jumbles, one letter to each square, to form six ordinary words.

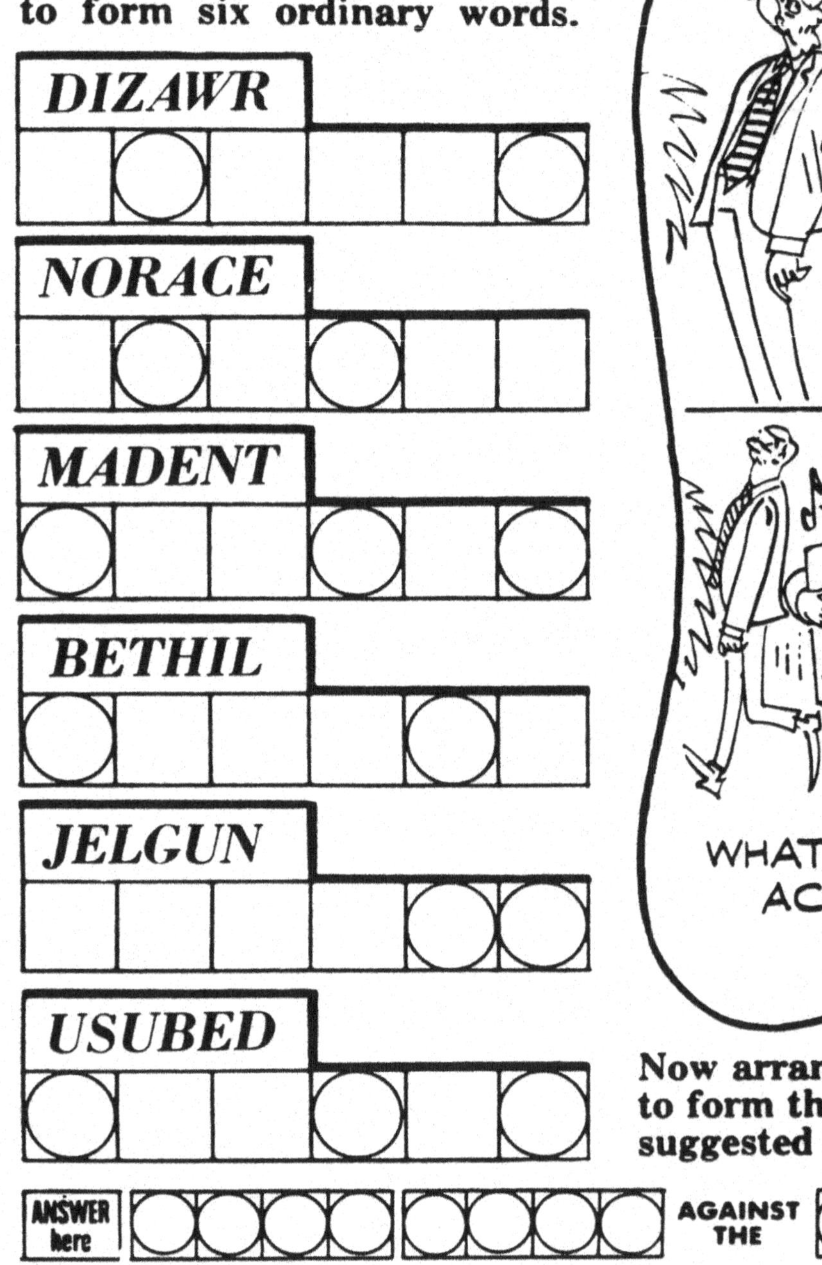
DIZAWR
NORACE
MADENT
BETHIL
JELGUN
USUBED

Don't trust him
Don't trust him
WHAT THE CUNNING ACCORDIONIST PLAYED.

Now arrange the circled letters to form the surprise answer, as suggested by the above cartoon.

ANSWER here: ☐☐☐☐ ☐☐☐☐ AGAINST THE ☐☐☐☐☐☐

166

JUMBLE®

Unscramble these six Jumbles, one letter to each square, to form six ordinary words.

DARAPE

MUNCOL

TABMIG

DUBOYE

GLANID

SHARTH

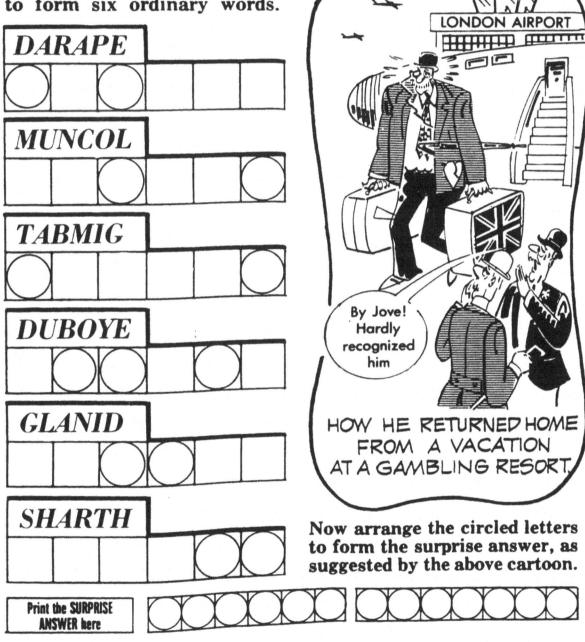

LONDON AIRPORT

By Jove! Hardly recognized him

HOW HE RETURNED HOME FROM A VACATION AT A GAMBLING RESORT

Now arrange the circled letters to form the surprise answer, as suggested by the above cartoon.

Print the SURPRISE ANSWER here

JUMBLE®

Unscramble these six Jumbles, one letter to each square, to form six ordinary words.

RETHOB

HERFIE

MOARRY

YULTIG

GRIFIN

NALTED

WHY IT CAN BE DANGEROUS TO TELL A PERSON A FUNNY STORY.

Now arrange the circled letters to form the surprise answer, as suggested by the above cartoon.

ANSWER here: HE MIGHT [ ][ ][ ][ ][ ] HIS [ ][ ][ ][ ] [ ][ ][ ]

JUMBLE®

Unscramble these six Jumbles, one letter to each square, to form six ordinary words.

ARPITE

KOECIO

SILENE

TINBAD

LURTIA

GRENED

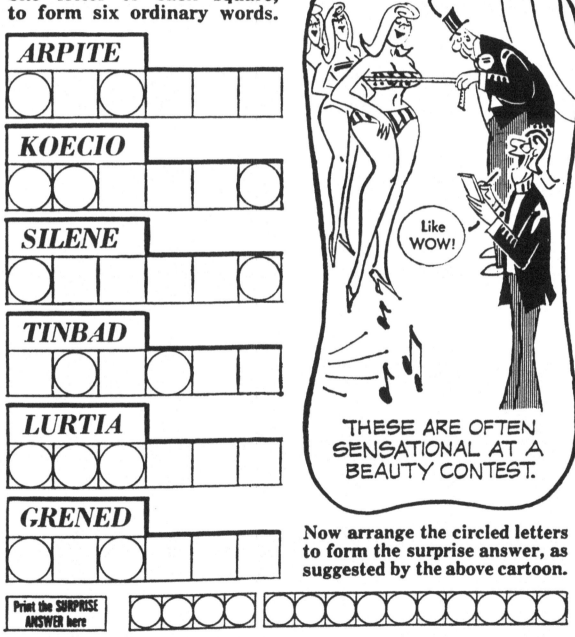

41 . . . 23 . . . 37 . . .
Like WOW!
THESE ARE OFTEN SENSATIONAL AT A BEAUTY CONTEST.

Now arrange the circled letters to form the surprise answer, as suggested by the above cartoon.

Print the SURPRISE ANSWER here

169

JUMBLE®

Unscramble these six Jumbles, one letter to each square, to form six ordinary words.

ZEFRYN

☐ ☐ ◯ ◯ ☐ ☐

NUGHAT

◯ ☐ ☐ ☐ ◯ ☐

MISOGE

☐ ☐ ◯ ☐ ◯ ☐

JELIAD

☐ ☐ ☐ ☐ ☐ ◯

GRATTE

◯ ☐ ☐ ☐ ☐ ◯

PARTUB

◯ ☐ ☐ ◯ ☐ ☐

GT1 = 48

10×10 =

5×5 =

$100

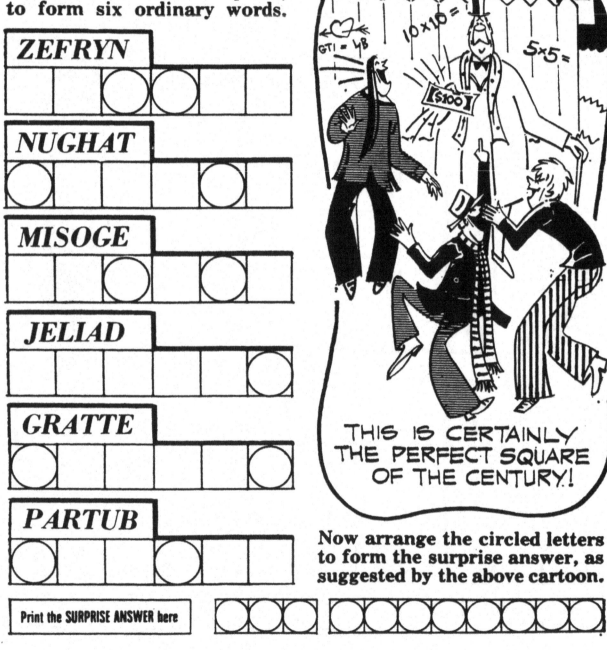

THIS IS CERTAINLY THE PERFECT SQUARE OF THE CENTURY!

Now arrange the circled letters to form the surprise answer, as suggested by the above cartoon.

Print the SURPRISE ANSWER here ◯◯◯ ◯◯◯◯◯◯◯◯

JUMBLE®

Unscramble these six Jumbles, one letter to each square, to form six ordinary words.

GININN

FEINED

CAUABS

DURECE

SQUOME

WHYROT

THIS MUSIC CAN GET YOU A GIRL.

Now arrange the circled letters to form the surprise answer, as suggested by the above cartoon.

Print the ANSWER here **THE** ○○○○○○○ ○○○○○

JUMBLE®

Unscramble these six Jumbles, one letter to each square, to form six ordinary words.

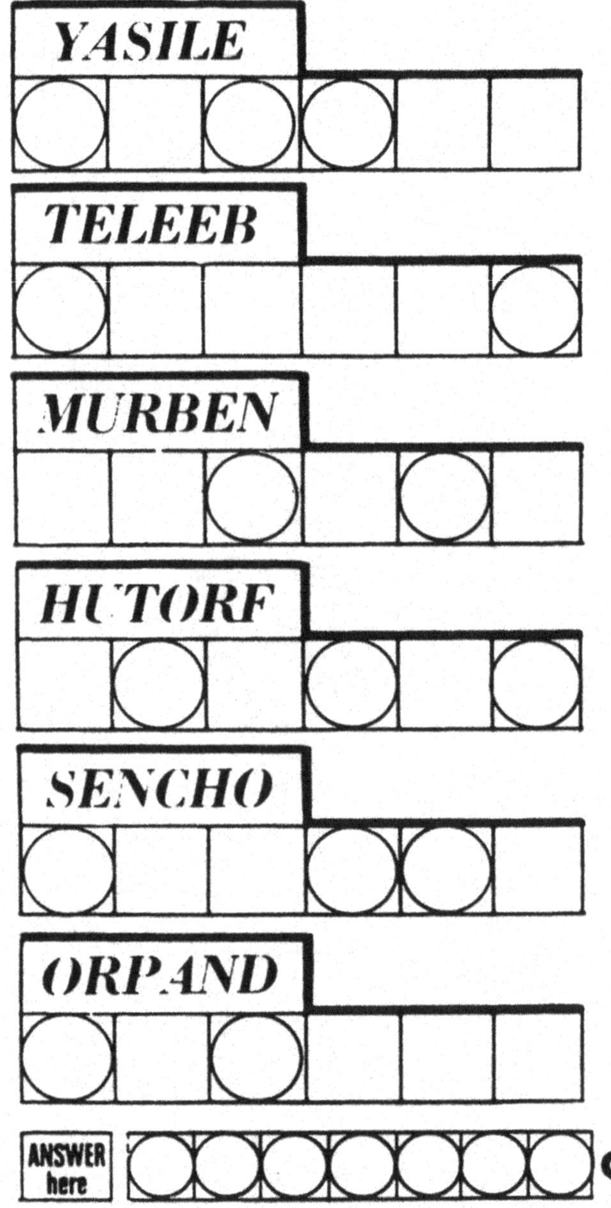

YASILE
TELEEB
MURBEN
HUTORF
SENCHO
ORPAND

You're late for church already
He'll hear from my lawyer
WHEN THE TAILOR WAS DELAYED, THE GROOM SUED HIM FOR THIS.

Now arrange the circled letters to form the surprise answer, as suggested by the above cartoon.

ANSWER here ○○○○○○○ OF ○○○○○○○○○

JUMBLE®

Unscramble these six Jumbles, one letter to each square, to form six ordinary words.

POEQUA

THALLE

LUDSON

TELSED

MARFOL

YONTUB

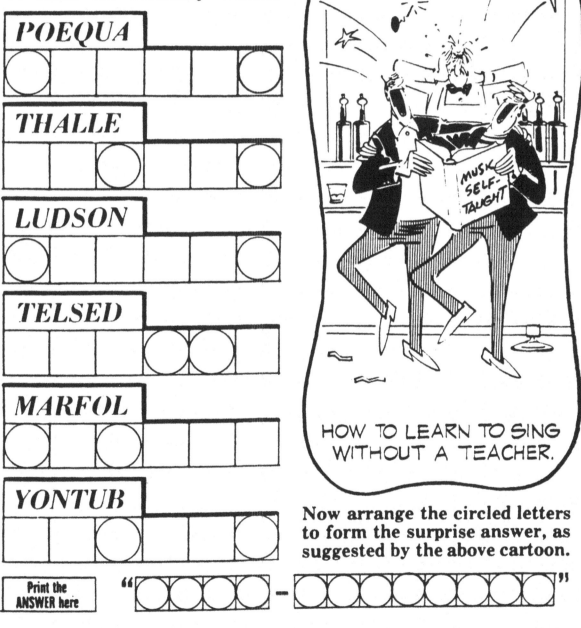

HOW TO LEARN TO SING WITHOUT A TEACHER.

Now arrange the circled letters to form the surprise answer, as suggested by the above cartoon.

Print the ANSWER here "____-________"

JUMBLE®

Unscramble these six Jumbles, one letter to each square, to form six ordinary words.

GLARAN

MORRAY

BUNNIO

MYSLOB

LIFTLE

IMMORE

BEER
Where to now?

A METRONOME CAN DETERMINE THE SPEED WITH WHICH YOU GO—

Now arrange the circled letters to form the surprise answer, as suggested by the above cartoon.

Print the SURPRISE ANSWER here

JUMBLE®

Unscramble these six Jumbles, one letter to each square, to form six ordinary words.

LAPEAT

DRAHLY

RANLEY

PAYNOC

ZEMENY

REVUIQ

BRAVO!
TERRIFIC!
GREAT!

WHAT APPLAUSE USUALLY IS.

Now arrange the circled letters to form the surprise answer, as suggested by the above cartoon.

PRINT YOUR ANSWER IN THE CIRCLES BELOW

THE "◯◯◯◯" OF ◯◯◯◯◯◯◯◯

175

JUMBLE®

Unscramble these six Jumbles, one letter to each square, to form six ordinary words.

WULTOA

LURBIA

TONOCY

DOUBIT

EXRILI

GITSAM

Thank you

Whew

Whew

Whew

Whew

WHAT TIME WAS IT WHEN HE FINISHED THE AFTER-DINNER SPEECH?

Now arrange the circled letters to form the surprise answer, as suggested by the above cartoon.

Print the SURPRISE ANSWER here: IT ( ) ( ) ( ) ( ) ( ) ( ) ( ) ( ) !

176

JUMBLE®

Unscramble these six Jumbles, one letter to each square, to form six ordinary words.

DEHEAB

YASQUE

FILRAY

WALCOL

ERASHE

NUCLUR

I'm out!

Hmmm—a straight

WHAT THE POKER-FACED POKER PLAYER HAD.

Now arrange the circled letters to form the surprise answer, as suggested by the above cartoon.

ANSWER here ◯ ◯◯◯◯◯ WITHOUT ◯ ◯◯◯◯◯

177

JUMBLE®

Unscramble these six Jumbles, one letter to each square, to form six ordinary words.

DUMEGS

HIALAD

CANTIO

OTTYNK

GRUFIE

PYRSOD

MAKE MUSIC—
AND NONSENSE!

Now arrange the circled letters to form the surprise answer, as suggested by the above cartoon.

Print the SURPRISE ANSWER here

!

178

JUMBLE®

Unscramble these six Jumbles, one letter to each square, to form six ordinary words.

YARVOS

GINDAR

BETASK

MIDYOF

VINTAY

LESUNS

On the house

On the house

On the house

HOW MUCH CAN A FREELOADER DRINK?

Now arrange the circled letters to form the surprise answer, as suggested by the above cartoon.

Print the SURPRISE ANSWER here

179

JUMBLE®

Unscramble these six Jumbles, one letter to each square, to form six ordinary words.

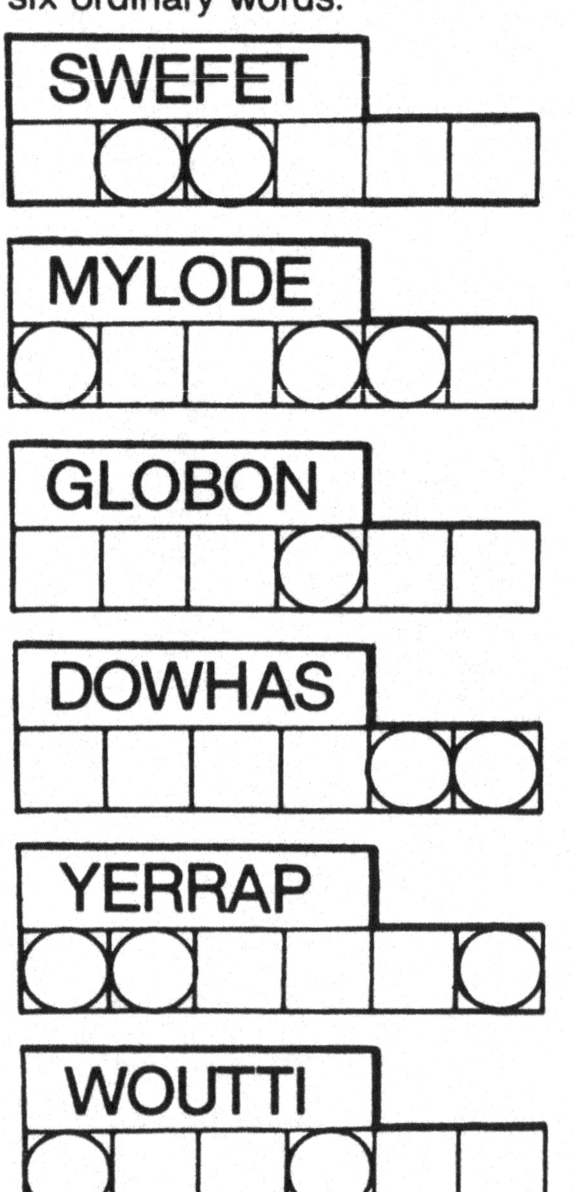
SWEFET
MYLODE
GLOBON
DOWHAS
YERRAP
WOUTTI

Don't repeat this, but. . .
WHAT A LADIES' LOUNGE MIGHT BE CALLED.

Now arrange the circled letters to form the surprise answer, as suggested by the above cartoon.

PRINT YOUR ANSWER IN THE CIRCLES BELOW

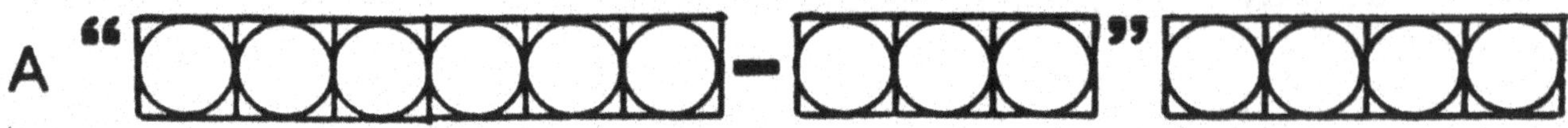
A " - "

180

JUMBLE®

Unscramble these six Jumbles, one letter to each square, to form six ordinary words.

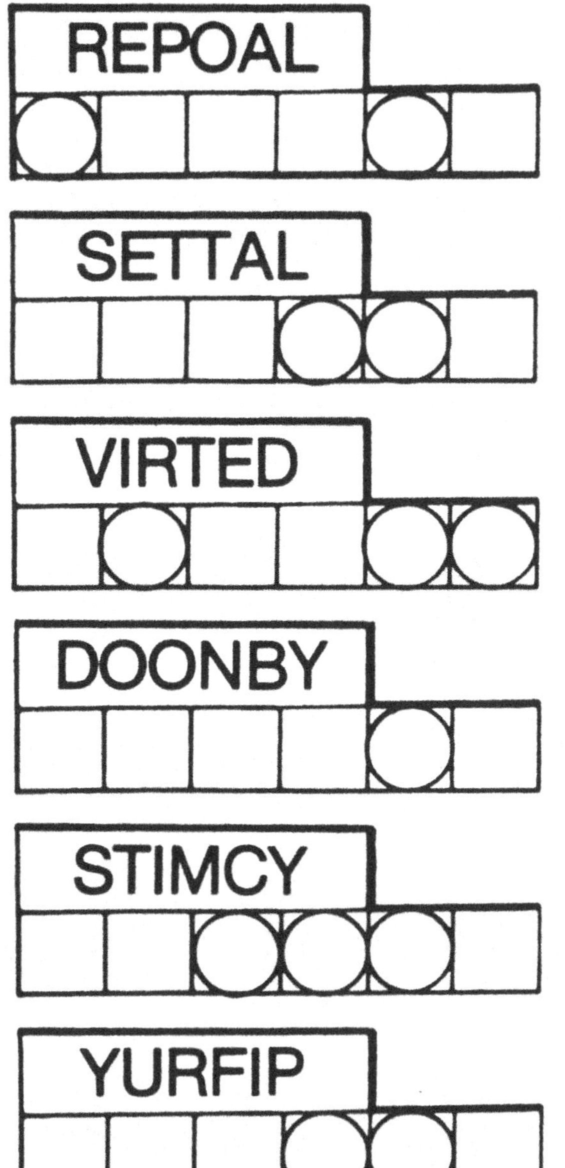
REPOAL
SETTAL
VIRTED
DOONBY
STIMCY
YURFIP

WHAT THAT TOAST GAVE RISE TO.

Now arrange the circled letters to form the surprise answer, as suggested by the above cartoon.

PRINT YOUR ANSWER IN THE CIRCLES BELOW

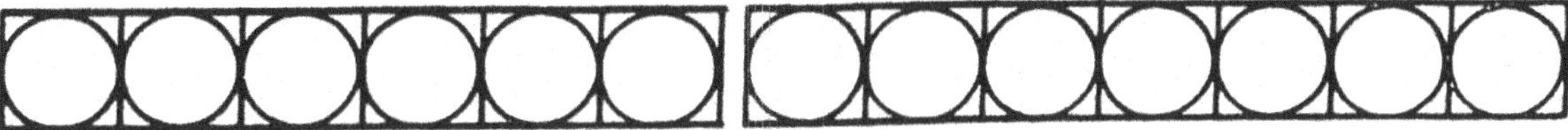

ANSWERS

1. **Jumbles**: TRULY WHISK SONATA VELVET
Answer: What gold diggers go for in order to get diamonds—HEARTS
2. **Jumbles**: PROBE WAGON JAGGED BUNKER
Answer: How you feel after a big weekend—WEAKENED
3. **Jumbles**: PRIOR TWINE DUPLEX RANDOM
Answer: What a man who couldn't hold his liquor did—DROPPED IT
4. **Jumbles**: CROAK PANSY BUNION GENTLE
Answer: What the nude show turned out to be—A PUT-ON
5. **Jumbles**: WOVEN BASIC DAINTY TEMPER
Answer: What the man who wore two suits to a masquerade party went as—TWINS
6. **Jumbles**: CRUSH PRUNE BLUING DISMAL
Answer: When you're this it's easy to feel chipper—IN THE CHIPS
7. **Jumbles**: NIPPY DAUNT SMUDGE TUXEDO
Answer: What the burlesque queen was responsible for—HER OWN "UNDOING"
8. **Jumbles**: HUSKY THYME FERVID COUSIN
Answer: What the poolroom hustler turned actor never missed—THE CUE
9. **Jumbles**: KEYED IVORY TYPIST MAINLY
Answer: When a bachelor gives a girl plenty of rope, this is how he might find himself—TIED IN A KNOT
10. **Jumbles**: OAKEN DITTO TRIBAL NUANCE
Answer: The best way to tell a woman's age—WHEN SHE'S NOT AROUND
11. **Jumbles**: BELIE YIELD INBORN GAITER
Answer: This might be the latest thing in weddings!—THE BRIDE
12. **Jumbles**: FOUNT VOCAL GYPSUM NOODLE
Answer: What they danced during the prison break—THE "CON-GO"
13. **Jumbles**: BEFIT FAKIR UNLOAD MUCOUS
Answer: What happened to the girl with the hourglass figure?—TIME RAN OUT
14. **Jumbles**: MOGUL GOUTY WEEVIL CASKET
Answer: What some weekend guests wear—OUT THEIR WELCOME
15. **Jumbles**: JOLLY IMBUE TACKLE PITIED
Answer: When open, it provides drinks—A BOTTLE
16. **Jumbles**: LYING BANAL MURMUR SALOON
Answer: When this happens you might expect a prearranged uprising to take place—THE ALARM RINGS
17. **Jumbles**: PAPER TOKEN FONDLY INVEST
Answer: What the gossip was—THE "KNIFE" OF THE PARTY
18. **Jumbles**: EIGHT LURID HUMBLE ALMOST
Answer: This might be used for self-protection at a sewing circle—A THIMBLE
19. **Jumbles**: GLADE CAPON BEFORE VELLUM
Answer: What you have when you spill beer on the stove—FOAM ON THE RANGE
20. **Jumbles**: ELATE SAUTE WHINNY HOOKED
Answer: What a gal who's on her toes keeps—AWAY FROM HEELS
21. **Jumbles**: CREEK ELUDE OBJECT GLOBAL
Answer: Why he couldn't tell that joke about oil—IT WAS TOO CRUDE
22. **Jumbles**: GRAVE BRIAR ZODIAC ASYLUM
Answer: What the jacket that caught fire must have been—A BLAZER
23. **Jumbles**: PRIME AZURE SPONGE EXPOSE
Answer: From a lorgnette you get this—A SNEER ON A SPEAR
24. **Jumbles**: CANAL GRIME HAIRDO SCHEME
Answer: This might mean cutting and cheating also—CHISELING
25. **Jumbles**: DUMPY BATCH MEASLY NOVICE
Answer: What the old-time brewers called their annual shindigs—"HOPS"
26. **Jumbles**: AFIRE GUILT BALSAM POETRY
Answer: What you might aim for in some circles—TARGETS
27. **Jumbles**: BANDY PARKA VIRILE CHUBBY
Answer: What people who drink to forget should do—PAY IN ADVANCE
28. **Jumbles**: YACHT NOISY DRUDGE FUMBLE
Answer: What a stag guest at the annual surgeons' dance said—MAY I CUT IN?
29. **Jumbles**: LYRIC FAVOR BUTANE MEDLEY
Answer: How the fat man spoke—BROADLY
30. **Jumbles**: EIGHT ABIDE METRIC BANANA
Answer: What happens when you encourage a gambler—YOU "A-BET" HIM
31. **Jumbles**: SUAVE HANDY POWDER LIQUID
Answer: What a top hat might make—YOUR HEAD SPIN
32. **Jumbles**: TABOO CHEEK BLUISH INDOOR
Answer: If it's still there, there isn't any—ACTION
33. **Jumbles**: COUGH HENNA FROLIC BYGONE
Answer: "Again in France?"—"ENCORE"
34. **Jumbles**: GLUEY JUMPY ASTHMA RADISH
Answer: She's a gem and much rarer than the mother of her—"PEARL"
35. **Jumbles**: CUBIT FOCUS POLITE BEAVER
Answer: There may be objections involved in the use of these words!—"BUTS"
36. **Jumbles**: MONEY BOUND FOMENT LADING
Answer: "Come out in the garden!"—"BLOOM"
37. **Jumbles**: TITLE AGONY GAINED EMBODY
Answer: What girls who play hard to get sometimes never do—GET GOT
38. **Jumbles**: AVAIL EMPTY JINGLE OPPOSE
Answer: Could be the result of a toss-up—what you should wear—"TAILS"
39. **Jumbles**: SUEDE NOVEL BALSAM ELICIT
Answer: What hot music does to people with "square" tastes—LEAVES THEM COLD
40. **Jumbles**: PROVE USURY TAMPER HORROR
Answer: What his stories had lots of—"RYE" HUMOR
41. **Jumbles**: AGONY TEMPO INVENT ATOMIC
Answer: What the trumpet player's girl friend accused him of doing—TOOT-TIMING HER
42. **Jumbles**: HAIRY DELVE EXPOSE CROUCH
Answer: "Here's how!"—in the kitchen—RECIPE
43. **Jumbles**: ARBOR FAUNA GUILTY BLEACH
Answer: This rather uncouth character has a couple of bars—A "BAR-BAR-IAN"
44. **Jumbles**: FILMY ABOVE GUITAR INVOKE
Answer: What he came into when he was born—BEING
45. **Jumbles**: OAKEN WHISK ARTFUL MASCOT
Answer: Agitated where cocktails are concerned—THE SHAKER
46. **Jumbles**: VOUCH BRAWL ERMINE CAVORT
Answer: A bad habit might get a "grip" on one—A "VICE"
47. **Jumbles**: AUGUR SYLPH LACKEY HAZARD
Answer: It requires an effort of will to leave it—A LEGACY

48. **Jumbles**: SOLAR LOATH IMPORT GENTLE
Answer: Sounds comfortably sick—"ILL AT EASE"

49. **Jumbles**: FOAMY KINKY NUTRIA CORNEA
Answer: Doesn't sound like preparation for war when they arm thus—"IN ARM" (arm in arm)

50. **Jumbles**: LOWLY SHEAF GALLEY FINITE
Answer: A kind of "art" you might be surprised to find in a moving picture—"STILL" LIFE

51. **Jumbles**: FACET CLUCK BOBBIN GENTRY
Answer: Inclined to be on the thin side—LEAN

52. **Jumbles**: UNWED FOLIO BARREL SURELY
Answer: It was awful—until a letter arrived to make it "legal"!—"L-AWFUL"

53. **Jumbles**: MEALY CUBIT NEARBY MODEST
Answer: Out of jail—and ill in bed—"B-AIL-ED"

54. **Jumbles**: COVEY GUMBO WALNUT OXYGEN
Answer: This room is just right for cocktails—"ELBOW" (elbow room)

55. **Jumbles**: METAL POACH WEEVIL CARNAL
Answer: "Just what's behind such painting?"—"THE WALL"

56. **Jumbles**: LOVER ABHOR FAULTY BARREN
Answer: What the fortune-teller said when asked how she felt about her work—I HAVE A BALL

57. **Jumbles**: FORCE BUMPY UNFOLD SCRIBE
Answer: What they all got during a party in the air raid shelter—"BOMBED"

58. **Jumbles**: GLORY SANDY ENGULF PRIMED
Answer: A singer "breaks down"—but recovers—"REGAINS"

59. **Jumbles**: JUROR WAKEN DROPSY HIATUS
Answer: What the architect turned actor certainly knew how to do—DRAW HOUSES

60. **Jumbles**: LATHE KEYED BEHIND COUSIN
Answer: "Disturbed" the sedate—"TEASED"

61. **Jumbles**: WAGON NEWSY ENTIRE IGUANA
Answer: What that attractive lady gambler had—WINNING WAYS

62. **Jumbles**: ANKLE NOOSE GRISLY AMPERE
Answer: Cake one might enjoy while taking a bath—SPONGE

63. **Jumbles**: UNITY ABBOT OPPOSE WALNUT
Answer: The king decided to have several court jesters so he could keep this—HIS WITS ABOUT HIM

64. **Jumbles**: LIVEN ALIAS INWARD DIVERT
Answer: She's an enthusiastic prima donna, whichever way you look at it—AN AVID DIVA

65. **Jumbles**: BILGE MOTIF LOTION FINISH
Answer: How people who live "loose" lives sometimes end up—"TIGHT"

66. **Jumbles**: LYRIC STUNG DOUBLE GOSPEL
Answer: What the prisoner who made music in his cell must have been—A "CELL-IST"

67. **Jumbles**: TONIC FLORA BESIDE MOTION
Answer: Might go to the head at a stag party—ANTLERS

68. **Jumbles**: RURAL DUCAL BRIDGE PERMIT
Answer: What pure art can produce—"RAPTURE"

69. **Jumbles**: IDIOM DERBY GRAVEN TARTAR
Answer: The card game the captain should stick to—"BRIDGE"

70. **Jumbles**: EIGHT TEPID BISHOP FIASCO
Answer: Two things that kept him from being a good dancer—HIS FEET

71. **Jumbles**: BUILT HOBBY CATCHY GAMBOL
Answer: Often opened by mistake—A BIG MOUTH

72. **Jumbles**: ARMOR LUNGE FAIRLY OBTUSE
Answer: Frequently keep people under the weather—UMBRELLAS

73. **Jumbles**: ABHOR SHINY INVENT PIRACY
Answer: A type of melody evidently requiring considerable effort—"STRAIN"

74. **Jumbles**: CHOKE SWOOP PERMIT TONGUE
Answer: What a man who drinks to forget often forgets—WHEN TO STOP

75. **Jumbles**: SKIMP COWER BARREL DENTAL
Answer: What the bartender who poured those extra big drinks was known as—THE "PLASTERER"

76. **Jumbles**: ESSAY PUPPY FACTOR DINGHY
Answer: This player "botched" his part—"HARPIST"

77. **Jumbles**: ENSUE FATAL CARBON JURIST
Answer: He tried to compose a drinking song but didn't make it past this—THE FIRST 2 BARS

78. **Jumbles**: COUGH IRATE AUTUMN FIDDLE
Answer: What time is it when clothes wear out?—RAGTIME

79. **Jumbles**: WHOOP CHIDE COLUMN FIXING
Answer: Language used by those pretentious jetsetters—HIGH-FLOWN

80. **Jumbles**: TOXIN MINUS HANGAR FIRING
Answer: What those boxers engaged in while having a few drinks—"INN" FIGHTING

81. **Jumbles**: CHESS UNWED MISERY WALNUT
Answer: She admitted she was forty but she didn't do this—SAY WHEN

82. **Jumbles**: CHIME GAUGE BOUNCE FALLOW
Answer: Some people who think they're very funny are really just this—LAUGHABLE

83. **Jumbles**: NUTTY SAUTE JACKAL ORATOR
Answer: What they told at the foot doctors' annual shindig—"CORNY" JOKES

84. **Jumbles**: BRAWL DUMPY HERALD RAGLAN
Answer: What it might be when you gambol across the street—A GAMBLE

85. **Jumbles**: KAPOK STOIC ORIOLE TOUCHY
Answer: A cowboy who talks first and thinks afterwards might do this—SHOOT FROM THE LIP

86. **Jumbles**: KEYED CURIO VESTRY CALLOW
Answer: What you can expect a smart cookie to be—A WISE "CRACKER"

87. **Jumbles**: APART POACH PAYOFF CHEERY
Answer: What they called the police officers' annual shindig—THE "COP HOP"

88. **Jumbles**: IMBUE SKULL UNCLAD SYMBOL
Answer: What the guy whose shoes squeaked must have had—MUSIC IN HIS "SOLE"

89. **Jumbles**: JETTY RAINY ADROIT CLEAVE
Answer: What the ballerina insisted that her partner do—"TOE" THE LINE

90. **Jumbles**: VOUCH IDIOM BRAZEN GROTTO
Answer: How did the trumpet player manage to get into that exclusive party?—HE "HORNED" IN

91. **Jumbles**: SNACK FLORA JUGGLE PEPTIC
Answer: What he who laughs last often doesn't do—GET THE JOKE

92. **Jumbles**: PORGY FRIAR HORROR ESTATE
Answer: "Did you hear my last joke?"—"I HOPE SO"

93. **Jumbles**: TROTH FOLIO IGUANA TUMULT
Answer: The impression made on one who's been in the Navy might be quite lasting—A TATTOO

94. **Jumbles**: PILOT MAGIC SPRUCE CENSUS
Answer: You'd get no praises from this—AN "ASPERSION"

95. **Jumbles**: GOOSE DEITY LICHEN INVERT
Answer: Much of the audience at that opera house was this—IN "TIERS" (tears)

96. **Jumbles**: ANKLE CAKED ENTIRE RADIUS
Answer: What a very repetitive type of dance might be called—A "REDUN-DANCE"

97. **Jumbles**: CHOKE PURGE LANCER HUMBLE
Answer: Something a woman finds easier to do with her face than with her mind—MAKE UP

98. **Jumbles**: GUISE ESSAY MENACE EXCISE
Answer: What some people enjoy drinking to—EXCESS

99. **Jumbles**: GOURD HIKER ALBINO BELLOW
Answer: What they said about that evening gown—"LOW!—& BEHOLD"

100. **Jumbles**: TONIC MOURN PULPIT BEACON
Answer: He became man of the hour because he knew how to make this—EVERY MINUTE COUNT

101. **Jumbles**: IRONY WAGER BEHOLD FARINA
Answer: What accordion music might sometimes be—LONG DRAWN OUT

102. **Jumbles**: CHAFF SUEDE HERMIT LOUNGE
Answer: What the soprano's "solo" was—"SO HIGH"

103. **Jumbles**: COUPE FORGO INTENT LOCKET
Answer: Always the center of attention—THE LETTER N

104. **Jumbles**: MONEY EXTOL UPLIFT LIZARD
Answer: They called the comedian a "gas" because he was this—JUST AN OLD "FUEL"

105. **Jumbles**: PRINT AMITY FEMALE HAIRDO
Answer: Talks without giving itself away—MONEY

106. **Jumbles**: HITCH ACRID ERMINE JURIST
Answer: What the violinist was up to—HIS CHIN IN MUSIC

107. **Jumbles**: VALVE CHEEK RABBIT BETRAY
Answer: How they greeted each other at the cardiologists' annual shindig—HEARTILY

108. **Jumbles**: IDIOM TAWNY ICEBOX SHERRY
Answer: What some people give when they lose their inhibitions—EXHIBITIONS

109. **Jumbles**: MURKY BARON EXHORT RADIUS
Answer: What a bridge player has to learn how to do—TAKE IT ON THE SHIN

110. **Jumbles**: EATEN GOOSE VERMIN EYELID
Answer: What some people do when they hold a conversation—NEVER LET GO

111. **Jumbles**: JEWEL FRANC BOTHER FEUDAL
Answer: If you're not careful about lending an ear you might get this—IT CHEWED OFF

112. **Jumbles**: SILKY VISTA CALICO ENTAIL
Answer: A "still" is an apparatus that makes many people this—"NOISY"

113. **Jumbles**: PHOTO FAMED DEFACE HALLOW
Answer: The best thing to have in a heated discussion—A COOL HEAD

114. **Jumbles**: BOOTY FORAY METRIC IMPEND
Answer: What some musical performances sound like someone's having—AN "OPERA-TION"

115. **Jumbles**: LINGO SORRY INDUCT BUNKER
Answer: He was so healthy it was this—"SICKENING"

116. **Jumbles**: TITLE AWARD YEARLY FERVID
Answer: A confirmed night owl is a man who stays up all night—DAY AFTER DAY

117. **Jumbles**: DOWNY HAVOC CANDID OBLIGE
Answer: What scandal has to be—BAD TO BE GOOD

118. **Jumbles**: DEITY ADULT FETISH BALLET
Answer: What "tales" told by a long-winded bore usually have too many of—"DE-TAILS"

119. **Jumbles**: FEVER MANLY BAKERY HEALTH
Answer: What they called that classy new art gallery—THE HALL OF FRAME

120. **Jumbles**: DITTO ALIAS LAUNCH BURLAP
Answer: What kind of jokes do those mountain folk tell?—"HILL-ARIOUS" ONES

121. **Jumbles**: ADULT HAVEN NEARLY EFFACE
Answer: What a good dancer has to be—"HANDY" WITH HIS FEET

122. **Jumbles**: MOUNT QUOTA AUBURN CAUGHT
Answer: That offensive talker had a tongue so sharp he almost did this—CUT HIS OWN THROAT

123. **Jumbles**: BILGE ABOUT RARELY FIDDLE
Answer: What a man given to horselaughs should be—"BRIDLED"

124. **Jumbles**: SIXTY OPERA JUSTLY HITHER
Answer: When you open your mouth to yawn, it could be a hint to others to do this—SHUT THEIRS

125. **Jumbles**: LOVER WINCE TYPHUS UNLESS
Answer: A scandalmonger is most happy when she confesses this—THE SINS OF OTHERS

126. **Jumbles**: COMET KNIFE JUNIOR QUARTZ
Answer: A guy should be this when he goes on a diet—QUIET

127. **Jumbles**: FELON TRYST COWARD SUBMIT
Answer: At most banquets this is the main course—DISCOURSE

128. **Jumbles**: TRULY BAKED JERSEY NIPPLE
Answer: What the audience gave him when he was expecting cheers—JEERS

129. **Jumbles**: SWOON GASSY NEGATE FARINA
Answer: The main course at the comedians' annual banquet—THE "ROAST"

130. **Jumbles**: FINNY PANIC GOSPEL CABANA
Answer: A person who seldom pays frequently finds that this is what his life style does—"PAYS"

131. **Jumbles**: CAPON ENTRY MUSLIN DRUDGE
Answer: He doesn't understand that his wife does—UNDERSTAND HIM

132. **Jumbles**: YOKEL OZONE MYOPIC GUTTER
Answer: "Society" was where young women started in by—"COMING OUT"

133. **Jumbles**: MOUSY SOUSE FIGURE TYCOON
Answer: One of the very few places where a woman might wear a hat these days—IN FRONT OF YOU

134. **Jumbles**: PATIO COUCH TURKEY SEPTIC
Answer: Saving one's face is often a matter of keeping—PART OF IT SHUT

135. **Jumbles**: IMPEL DOILY JERSEY INLAND
Answer: A person who is constantly giving others a piece of his mind usually has this—NONE TO SPARE

136. **Jumbles**: FLUTE VIXEN TRUANT PREACH
Answer: The best way to make a long story short—INTERRUPT HIM

137. **Jumbles**: GIANT BASIN OBTUSE TALLOW
Answer: Often drunk but never intoxicated—A TOAST

138. **Jumbles**: KNOWN AWFUL LAYOFF MAKEUP
Answer: He found it easier to sit tight than this—WALK THAT WAY

139. **Jumbles**: ORBIT BLOOM TONGUE LEEWAY
Answer: Their old man made money in questionable ways, and now they're enjoying this—"WILL-GOTTEN" GAINS

140. **Jumbles**: SAUTE DRYLY CUPFUL PLURAL
Answer: What they call a lot of crumbs held together by their own dough—THE UPPER CRUST

141. **Jumbles**: EPOCH AFTER FASTEN MALICE
Answer: A self-indulgent guy never does this—"NO" HIMSELF

142. **Jumbles**: EXERT RAINY DOMINO SCARCE
Answer: Many a woman thinks she is fond of sports until she does this—MARRIES ONE

143. **Jumbles**: DRONE HEDGE BROOCH HOURLY
Answer: What the baker turned comedian knew how to make—DOUGH OUT OF "CORN"

144. **Jumbles**: PROVE METAL FETISH SHANTY
Answer: What they call that guy who always remains at a party after the food and drink are all gone—THE HOST

145. **Jumbles**: LEGAL HYENA VASSAL FEEBLE
Answer: Some fashions are cut to this—"SEE" LEVEL

146. **Jumbles**: GAVEL CIVIL LARYNX FAUCET
Answer: Some people who go "all out" often end up—"ALL IN"

147. **Jumbles**: PUTTY GROIN DEVICE MASCOT
Answer: The opportunist has no use for friends—HE CAN'T "USE"

148. **Jumbles**: BATON USURP POLLEN NOUGAT
Answer: That opinionated guy was always down on anything—HE WAS NOT "UP" ON

149. **Jumbles**: IVORY WEIGH MISLAY IMPUGN
Answer: That pathological liar tells the truth only when his—LIPS AREN'T MOVING

150. **Jumbles**: OZONE TIGER ASYLUM RITUAL
Answer: What some music gets when you're dining at a patriotic banquet—A RISE OUT OF YOU

151. **Jumbles**: FOIST ESSAY ASTRAY BUBBLE
Answer: He climbed out of his "status quo" in order to improve this—HIS STATUS

152. **Jumbles**: WEARY SHEAF HUNTER CHISEL
Answer: A good poker player conceals the kind of hand he has by the kind of face—HE HASN'T

153. **Jumbles**: HABIT MINER LIKELY FROSTY
Answer: He's a person about whom you'll never hear a good word, unless you hear—HIM TALK ABOUT HIMSELF

154. **Jumbles**: HITCH AGLOW OMELET SINFUL
Answer: Success hasn't gone to his head yet—JUST TO HIS MOUTH

155. **Jumbles**: STUNG ABIDE COUPLE TOWARD
Answer: A short "cutting" remark may be expressed in these—"BLUNT" WORDS

156. **Jumbles**: HOUSE TRACT EYEFUL PHYSIC
Answer: He always accompanied his wife to the opera, whether he needed this or not—THE SLEEP

157. **Jumbles**: WOVEN EXPEL CRAVAT SYMBOL
Answer: Some people who attend conventions rarely do this—OBSERVE ANY

158. **Jumbles**: CRESS ANKLE BAKING EMBRYO
Answer: At wild parties "anything goes," and the first is usually this—MANNERS

159. **Jumbles**: MINUS SEIZE HALLOW STOLEN
Answer: A fortune hunter doesn't really care for a woman's company unless—SHE OWNS IT

160. **Jumbles**: SAVOR ENEMY BEFALL RATIFY
Answer: A real friend knocks before he enters—NOT AFTER HE LEAVES

161. **Jumbles**: RIVET CROAK PUZZLE DIVERT
Answer: What they gave that gloomy looking guy at the party—THE "DOUR" PRIZE

162. **Jumbles**: AORTA POKED JINGLE DIGEST
Answer: That grouch spreads good cheer wherever—HE DOESN'T GO

163. **Jumbles**: TWINE NUDGE EMBARK DOMINO
Answer: What life was for the barfly—JUST "MEET" & DRINK

164. **Jumbles**: CHIME SAUTE PALACE THRASH
Answer: People who refuse to wear their prescribed eyeglasses sometimes make this of themselves—SPECTACLES

165. **Jumbles**: WIZARD CORNEA TANDEM BLITHE JUNGLE SUBDUE
Answer: What the cunning accordionist played—BOTH ENDS AGAINST THE MIDDLE

166. **Jumbles**: PARADE COLUMN GAMBIT BUOYED LADING THRASH
Answer: How he returned home from a vacation at a gambling resort—POUNDS LIGHTER

167. **Jumbles**: BOTHER HEIFER ARMORY GUILTY FIRING DENTAL
Answer: Why it can be dangerous to tell a person a funny story—HE MIGHT LAUGH HIS HEAD OFF

168. **Jumbles**: PIRATE COOKIE SENILE BANDIT RITUAL GENDER
Answer: These are often sensational at a beauty contest—TAPE RECORDINGS

169. **Jumbles**: FRENZY NAUGHT EGOISM JAILED TARGET ABRUPT
Answer: This is certainly the perfect square of the century!—TEN THOUSAND

170. **Jumbles**: INNING DEFINE ABACUS REDUCE MOSQUE WORTHY
Answer: This music can get you a girl—THE WEDDING MARCH

171. **Jumbles**: EASILY BEETLE NUMBER FOURTH CHOSEN PARDON
Answer: When the tailor was delayed, the groom sued him for this—PROMISE OF BREECHES

172. **Jumbles**: OPAQUE LETHAL UNSOLD ELDEST FORMAL BOUNTY
Answer: How to learn to sing without a teacher—"DUET-YOURSELF"

173. **Jumbles**: RAGLAN ARMORY BUNION SYMBOL FILLET MEMOIR
Answer: A metronome can determine the speed with which you go—FROM BAR TO BAR

174. **Jumbles**: PALATE HARDLY NEARLY CANOPY ENZYME QUIVER
Answer: What applause usually is—THE "ZEAL" OF APPROVAL

175. **Jumbles**: OUTLAW BURIAL TYCOON OUTBID ELIXIR STIGMA
Answer: What time was it when he finished the after-dinner speech?—IT WAS ABOUT TIME!

176. **Jumbles**: BEHEAD QUEASY FAIRLY CALLOW HEARSE UNCURL
Answer: What the poker-faced poker player had—A FLUSH WITHOUT A BLUSH

177. **Jumbles**: SMUDGE DAHLIA ACTION KNOTTY FIGURE DROPSY
Answer: Make music—and nonsense!—FIDDLESTICKS!

178. **Jumbles**: SAVORY DARING BASKET MODIFY VANITY UNLESS
Answer: How much can a freeloader drink?—ANY GIVEN AMOUNT

179. **Jumbles**: FEWEST MELODY OBLONG SHADOW PRAYER OUTWIT
Answer: What a ladies' lounge might be called—A "POWWOW-DER ROOM"

180. **Jumbles**: PAROLE LATEST DIVERT NOBODY MYSTIC PURIFY
Answer: What that toast gave rise to—LIFTED SPIRITS